Caring for

ELDERLY
PARENTS

Caring for
ELDERLY PARENTS

· **Ruth Whybrow** ·

A Crossroad Book
The Crossroad Publishing Company
New York

1996

The Crossroad Publishing Company
370 Lexington Avenue, New York, NY 10017

Copyright © 1996 by Ruth Whybrow

Printed in the United States of America

Photo credit: Kate Siepmann

Library of Congress Cataloging-in-Publication Data

Whybrow, Ruth.
    Caring for elderly parents / Ruth Whybrow.
        p. cm.
    ISBN 0-8245-1558-7 (pbk.)
    1. Aging parents – Care – United States. 2. Adult children – United
States. 3. Intergenerational relations – United States.
4. Caregivers – United States. I. Title.
HV1461.W498   1996
362.6 – dc20   96-20820
                                                                     CIP

To my parents,
Doris and George Steele

Contents

Acknowledgments

This book has grown out of my work with older people and their families. I have met them as individuals in my office, in groups, in workshops. In telling me what they need and what they wish for, and in letting me into their struggles, pains, and satisfactions, they have all contributed to this book. I owe them much and thank them.

With friends, colleagues, and even strangers, I find that concerns about elderly parents are an increasingly frequent subject of conversation. These too have taught me much. I would especially like to thank Nancy Crumbine, Gretchen Holm, Miriam Holm, Audrey Logan, Donella Meadows, Dena Romero, Kate Siepmann, John Trethaway, and Peter Whybrow for their suggestions, encouragement, and personal experiences.

Above all, my appreciation goes to two people — Helen Whybrow and Kate Siepmann. Helen's enthusiasm and professional advice in the early days, when I most needed them, were essential. Without her, this book may never have started. Without Kate, the quality of this book would be less. Generously, she has given her time and editorial skills to push me toward a smoother style and greater clarity. I am grateful to them both.

Introduction

ᡄ᠍ᡲ

W ATCHING OUR PARENTS grow old is difficult. Their old age is a landmark — for us as well as for them — as we all enter new territory for which no good map exists. What hazards lie ahead? We are uncertain but, sensing no good, are often afraid of the answer. We dread our parents' decline, imagine their unhappiness, anticipate their need for us, grieve that we will eventually be without them, and, most of all, fear what this means for our own lives. Our questions are numerous and the answers are often elusive.

Over many years as a psychiatric social worker, I have met and talked with adult children as they try to decide what is best for their ailing parents and themselves. They face a complicated equation — balancing on one side, their own needs, responsibilities, and abilities, and, on the other, those of their parents. All too often the children experience distress as the needs of their parents begin to outweigh and strain their own capacities.

For the first time in our history, children can expect that their parents will reach advanced old age. The biblical "three score and ten years" is no longer the expected end of a life's span but a mere stepping stone as unprecedented numbers pass into the decades beyond. More people reach the age of eighty now than ever before. One of the less heralded implications of this explosion in numbers is that more and more adult children have some degree of responsibility for one, two or, with in-laws, possibly three or four elderly relatives. All old people do not become frail or needy, but the specter of physical and mental deterioration looms larger as the years advance. Even while parents are healthy and independent, their children watch with some apprehension, thankful that they are doing so well, but alert for any sign of failure. Many children who have already stepped into the realm of their parents' decline find themselves faced with new responsibilities that were not part of their life's plan and for which their other commitments leave little room.

"How do I take care of my parent?" was a question not generally asked before now. In the "old days," the parents who did reach old age were usually cared for by several children, most of whom

11

lived nearby. Government took responsibility only for the indigent, leaving families with no option but to care for their own. Today, the circumstances are more complex. Along with an increased life span have come other demographic, social, and political changes, creating situations that can complicate a family's ability to provide care. The elderly are not only more numerous but older, and they have more chronic illnesses. Their children are fewer, live farther away, and for the first time in history, most daughters work outside the home.

One thing has *not* changed: it is still families who supply the primary emotional and practical support for their relatives, far outweighing help from any other source. People continue to care for, and about, their own. Almost three times as many disabled older people are supported in their own homes by their kin as live in nursing homes. The vast majority of older parents see at least one of their children once each week. Whether families assume responsibility with love or a sigh of inevitability, with affection or resentment, out of concern or a sense of duty, they invariably answer, "Will I take on this care?" in the affirmative. The question they grapple with is "How can I manage to meet my parents' needs?"

Helping older parents inevitably comes at a cost. For adult children, the price is often high. Many of the clients who come to talk to me describe themselves as feeling fatigued, irritable, tense, and vaguely unwell, as they face the physical demands and emotional upheaval of their parents' decline. Caring for older relatives does not *replace* other responsibilities; it *adds* to them. Most care is provided by women, especially daughters (and often daughters-in-law), all of whom already fill many roles in their family, community, and workplace. Often described as the "generation in the middle" — with their own children and their parents both looking to them for some help — these people have to find reservoirs of time and energy where, in most cases, no surplus exists.

Parents' needs come in many shapes and forms, as do their children's abilities to respond. Stress emerges when the need outruns the resources, when the demands for time, energy, patience, or compassion are more than children can meet. The level of stress varies from person to person, from situation to situation, but it is always significant.

Along with my clients, I have learned that there are no simple answers. The demands on them and the questions they face are not resolved by any single formula or list of services. Factual information and resources — whether financial, medical, or social — can be invaluable but will yield only partial answers. Beyond amassing such information, we have to puzzle about what help our parents require, what they will accept, and what, given our circumstances, it is possible for us to do.

At a more profound and sometimes painful level, we have to recognize that our feelings about our parents, both present and past, will affect the nature and quality of the care that we can provide. Whether we like our parents, whether we and our brothers and sisters can work together, whether our spouse is supportive, whether our children need much of our attention, all affect our ability as caregivers. Questions become dilemmas as we struggle with these complex layers of competing obligations, conflicting loyalties, mixed feelings, and varying levels of affection. The resolution of these dilemmas is different for each of us.

Despite the difficulties, there are answers to be found. It is my intent to make the search easier. This book is for adult children who either face the reality that their parents need help, or the prospect that they soon will. Whatever your economic or social position, your race or religion, or your economic resources, when your parents begin to fail you all have many concerns in common. We will explore many of these concerns. It is possible to help your parents without becoming depressed or overwhelmed. Indeed, you will be much more effective if you feel reasonably content with what you are doing. One of my hopes is to give you some insights and choices that will help you achieve the balance that meets both your parents' needs and your own. Clarity of vision does not remove difficulties but, with eyes open, we are all more able to avoid pitfalls and make more thoughtful decisions. Awareness does not eliminate pain or concern, but with it we can be more honest with ourselves and members of our family. With that honesty, we have the basis for working together on one of life's most compelling issues.

One of my beliefs, based on my own and others' experience, is that the challenge of facing our parents' old age can bring opportunities for growth and change within ourselves. Old age is not merely diminishment. Good things can and do happen. Of the countless people I have worked with, most find that, despite difficulties, they are ultimately enriched by the experience of caring for their parents. Relationships may deepen, rifts in your family may heal, you may have the satisfaction of fulfilling an obligation, of giving help where it is needed, or of meeting a challenge that stretches and teaches you in ways you never thought possible. Increased contact with your parents as they move to the end of their lives brings its own stress, but at the same time it may also enable you to fully express your love and complete your relationship with these people who have been so important to you.

This book is focused on specific dilemmas faced by adult children as their parents begin to fail. Each chapter addresses a particular issue, using personal anecdotal material to illustrate the text, which explores a wider range of questions, alternative solutions, and recommendations. The case histories are composites of numerous people I have known.

The information I present comes from several sources. Primarily, it is drawn from my experience as a psychotherapist, working individually and in groups with adults of all ages. Many of my clients are elderly; others seek advice about their elderly parents. From these people I have learned a great deal. The elderly and their families have become a rich field of study for researchers and gerontologists in recent years, and my reading of this professional literature supplements my personal experience.

Chapter 1 introduces the variety of feelings — some expected, some surprising — that you may experience as you find your parents can no longer manage alone. These feelings and your awareness of them are important because they influence how you will meet the challenge of your parents' aging. This chapter introduces a number of case histories, most of which becomes the focus of a subsequent chapter.

Chapter 2 describes the experience of growing old — what changes occur, what remains the same, what is myth, what is reality. Though people are more diverse in their old age than at any other age, and your parents are different in countless ways from others of their age, there is some information that is important for you to know.

Chapter 3 explores a common dilemma. How do you know when your parents need help? Some parents can be clear about what they need, but more often the situation is complex. Your parents may hide their difficulties, or, conversely, they may express their distress all too readily. More confusing yet, they may be incapable of recognizing that they can no longer manage on their own. You may live so far away that it is difficult to assess the situation. How do you decide whether they have a problem, whether there is a solution, and, most difficult of all, if or when you should step in?

Having decided that your parent needs help, what next? Given your circumstances, what are the reasonable choices? *Chapter 4* addresses the factors you should take into account and how to go about implementing your decision in a way that gives the best chance of a satisfactory outcome.

"What do I say?" is the subject of *Chapter 5*. Communication is a vital component of all relationships, and no less so with elderly parents. Their old age requires a new sensitivity on your part. If you are to be effective, you need to have a sense of what your parents are thinking and feeling. How do you talk about uncomfortable subjects, such as living alone, or facing death? How do you communicate when brain trauma, such as Alzheimer's disease or stroke, strips your parent of the ability to use or understand words?

Chapter 6 addresses your other family relationships, especially those with brothers and sisters. Unfortunately, they are often more a source of tension than help. Whether you are the child primarily responsible for your parents or the one who lives at a distance, we will explore ways of being supportive of each other and working constructively together.

Chapter 7 describes a number of problems that, while not an inevitable part of aging, occur with enough regularity to warrant mention. These include hearing loss, forgetfulness, depression, reactions to hospitalization, and medication.

Chapter 8 asks "What are the limits?" Are your expectations of yourself and your relationship with your parent realistic? What do you do when you do not like your parent, when you are burned out, when you have reached your limit?

Like most challenges, your parents' old age is an opportunity for personal growth. *Chapter 9* focuses on what you can do to improve the quality of your relationship with your parents and your siblings.

The final *Chapter 10* brings you to the end of your parents' lives and the process of grieving, of letting go, and living your life beyond them.

🌿

As you watch your parents struggle with the losses of old age and as they look to you for assistance, you face a difficult and often painful situation. If you choose to help, you may often feel unhappy, trapped, and overwhelmed by the additional responsibilities. You will wrestle with dilemmas that will appear to have no good solution.

The stress, the work, the grief and frustrations are real. But there are ways of lightening your burden, or at least of making it less onerous. Along with hardships you may also experience moments of deep affection for your parents, closeness to your siblings, and a satisfying sense of previously untapped strengths in yourself.

Your circumstances are not exactly like those of any other person. Your responsibilities, your personality, your relationship with your parent are unique. At the same time, you have much in common with all adult children concerned about their aging parents. You are not alone. Others have faced the same difficult questions, felt similar feelings, and explored the unfamiliar territory ahead of you. I have distilled the experiences many have shared with me and present them here both as a practical guide in your search for answers and as emotional support on your particular journey.

· Chapter 1 ·

Charting the Emotional Landscape

❧

A GROUP of a dozen people, mostly women, one couple, and one single man had come to my seminar on "Aging Parents." They all had concerns or questions about their elderly parents and were hoping for some ideas to help them deal with their situations. I knew from experience that they were uncomfortable, half-wishing they were not there. I also knew that in two hours they would leave this first session relieved they had found others who understood what they were going through.

My first goal was to help them understand what they were feeling as they saw their parents growing older and more needy. To begin identifying some of these feelings I presented a fictional situation and asked for their reactions.

The telephone rings. It's the neighbor of your eighty-year-old mother who lives a hundred miles away. She tells you that your mother has just fallen. She's not seriously hurt — just bruised. You ought to know, though, that this is not the first time that she's been found on the floor. In general she's not been doing well recently. Perhaps, the neighbor hinted, you should do something.

There was a prolonged silence. Then words came tumbling out: "anger," "guilt," "sadness," "helplessness," "overwhelmed." People talked at the same time, frequently voicing the same concerns. As the flurry of reactions subsided, a woman who had not yet spoken said "I feel all those things. I'm pulled in so many directions, I sometimes don't know what to think." Others nodded in agreement. Although everyone's situation was different, each shared similar feelings.

17

Honest Assessments

Helping parents is not just a matter of organizing resources and making practical decisions. Finances, living space, health, and physical distance are some of the many important factors in determining the type and amount of help you can give. But possibly more important are emotional factors, such as the quality of your relationship and your and your parents' ability to give and receive care. Emotional obstacles, as well as physical ones, can create troubling situations. If your parent is critical and you tend to become demoralized, you may be uncomfortable spending much time together. Conversely, positive feelings between you and your parents can diminish the practical obstacles you face.

When your parents become sick or frail, you feel a variety of emotions, many of which are intense, some quite painful. They are not to be ignored. All feelings — responsibility, anger, affection, resentment — become major factors influencing what you do, how you do it, and how effective you are. The more you recognize what you are feeling, the better prepared you will be and the more likely to make positive choices both for yourself and your parents.

Most people's feelings toward their parents in old age are similar to those they had when growing up. If you had a relationship that was companionable and affectionate for the most part, it is likely to remain so. If it was predominantly conflict-ridden or distant, it is unlikely much will have changed. This may seem to be stating the obvious, but it is often overlooked when we consider ourselves in relation to our aged parents. In our effort to be helpful and responsible, all of us — children and parents — may not take a realistic look at the quality of our relationship and, when failing to do so, make mistakes that could have been avoided. At a deep level, we are invested in convincing ourselves that we can get along well. Now, as adults, with our parents old, we hope — surely — the difficulties of the past will remain in the past.

Most of us find, however, that old patterns survive intact. The balance of power shifts if children become physically and mentally more competent in some areas than their parents, but the qualities of relationship — close or distant, comfortable or abrasive, respectful or authoritarian — remain the same. A son as an adult, for example, may be able to overwhelm his father in an argument in a way not possible when he was a child, but his feelings of being opposed or disapproved of are still there to dilute any sense of victory.

Under some circumstances, however, the feelings that you and your parents have for each other may change significantly — for better or worse. As people grow old, personalities may alter, and certain characteristics become emphasized. Disease, loss, and worry take their toll and may change an outgoing, independent person into one who seems self-centered and pessimistic. The pains and burdens of old age test the sweetest and strongest among us. On the other hand, some of you may find your older parents easier to love. A parent who has always been domineering and critical may mellow with age.

Children change too. Experiences during your life affect your tolerance, empathy, and willingness to give to others. As the circumstances within your family shift, you, your parents, and your brothers and sisters will all be able to adapt if you build on the strengths in each other and let go of past grievances and disappointments. With effort, positive change is usually possible. I have found that it depends on the level of honest self-awareness you have or are able to develop. When you are able to look inside yourself and recognize that neither difficulties nor solutions are created only by your parents or your siblings, then you can do much to help the situation.

Why Can't I Fix This?

Jack was first to speak. His response to my fictional story was one of irritation.

Why don't old people see these situations coming and do something about them before they turn into a crisis? My own mother and father might have got into a similar fix if I hadn't been keeping an eye on them.

The whole last year has been tough, but I think I did the right thing by persuading my parents to move. They had been living in the same big old house for forty years and were clearly unable to maintain it or even make a comfortable life for themselves. Here's an example: my father, who can scarcely walk, insisted he could mow his own lawn. It was ridiculous for a man in his eighties to be cutting grass. But he refused to see that. So, rather than employ someone, he'd exhaust himself and let my mother worry about him having a heart attack.

It was obvious to all of us that they had to move into a smaller place, more modern and manageable, but they seemed incapable of actually deciding to do it. I finally found the perfect solution — I thought — a condo, near to me and with no grass to mow. Well, they got all moved in — it's a nice community, with plenty of things to do — but do you think they're taking advantage of it? I get so annoyed at their passivity. It's as if they are refusing to get back into life, go out and meet people, get involved. I feel I've done the best I can do for them; I visit them every week, and they come to our house for Sunday lunch now and then. It's not that they ask for more from me — they don't and I'm glad — but unless I do more, taking them places, introducing them to people, I don't think they'll ever be happy here.

As you face your parents' old age, you have little experience to draw on; the situation is entirely new. If you are lucky you may have a friend involved with aging parents, but more often you are on your own, feeling helpless about which questions to ask, let alone which solutions to suggest. What should I look for? What services exist? What are my parents' needs, expectations, fears, hopes?

To make matters worse, we are often taken in by clichés about aging that are rarely useful and often downright false: "Older people become senile if they live long enough." "Older people are inflexible and unable to make changes." "Old people are self-centered."

Most of us try to imagine how we would react in our parents' situation. To an extent this makes us more sensitive to their position, but, in reality, our feelings may be very different. Putting ourselves in another person's shoes, however well intentioned, only tells us what *we* would do in that situation. To be actually helpful, we need to know more of what *the other* is feeling. Jack knows what he would think about mowing the lawn if he were his father, but that isn't the point. He needs to be able to see it from his father's point of view. For his father, grass-cutting was not a chore to avoid. It was a sign that he was still independent, competent, and in control.

Our ideas about how our parents should live and cope with their problems may have little to do with what our parents want for themselves. It is useful to have some facts, not myths, about aging in general. But the really relevant knowledge comes from understanding what our parents are feeling, what is important to them with their unique values, hopes, and fears.

Another way we deal with helplessness is to take action for action's sake. It is as if doing something — anything — is preferable to doing nothing. It makes us feel better to take control, for the moment at least. It may not be helpful to our parents, however, or to anyone else, in the long run. Sometimes "help" may be misguided and make a bad situation worse.

When I was a student social worker, my first client was an elderly man referred to me by his doctor because he was reluctant to leave the hospital. Physically, he had made a good recovery from a stroke; there was no reason medically why he should not be discharged. When I visited him on the ward, he seemed pleased for the company. He was shy at first but soon told me that he had lived alone since his wife died a year ago. He dreaded returning to his lonely apartment. Naively, I offered him a number of practical solutions, including joining the local men's club. When we met next, he was polite but noticeably more distant. My supervisor pointed out that I did not know my client well enough to make such suggestions, and in doing so, I had fallen into the category of people who failed to understand him. Fortunately, he gave me a second chance. He was subsequently able to share his grief at his wife's death and, only then, was ready to explore for himself some ways that might ease his loneliness.

Like my client, your parents are struggling with the loss of something they valued — health, home, spouse — which can never be fully replaced however hard you or they try. You are indeed helpless to make a perfect repair. At best, the solution is a serviceable alternative, acceptable in the given circumstances. You have to accept that you do not have the power to make your parents' lives as they once were.

Shouldering the Load

Martha heaved a sigh of recognition as she listened to my anecdote.

My mother had a stroke two years ago. We'd always been close, and when it came time to take care of her, it never occurred to me that anyone else would do it but me. My mother had taken care of her mother — she lived with us and I have really happy memories of coming home from school to find her and the cookies she baked. I have three brothers and they're great about helping with Mom — one has taken over her finances, the others take her for vacations — but I think it was always assumed by all of us that I'd have the primary responsibility. And I wouldn't have it any other way. We're still close, still have cozy chats when I come home from work.

I just feel I should be doing it better, making less heavy weather of it somehow. I get up earlier than I used to so I can help Mom wash and dress. Then I fix her some lunch and leave it in the fridge. My kids are terrific about checking on her after school, but I don't want them to feel weighted down by any sense of duty. My husband has been very supportive too, though he more and more frequently points out that I'm tense, or overdoing it. It seems to me that my mother managed having three generations in the one house with unruffled, good-natured calm. I'm not so good at it. I know I'm irritable quite often, and I've started getting headaches more than I used to. And I can't figure out why I'm not coping better. After all, I'm lucky, with my mother easy to get on with and my family helpful. I shouldn't even need to be at this group. Managing my job and giving the kind of attention I want to all the members of my family shouldn't be so difficult. I just keep feeling like I'm coming up short.

Most of you, like Martha, feel some degree of responsibility for your parents as they age. This is as true today as of any generation. We hear so much about the demise of the American family — that people do not care for each other as in times past. This is another myth; in fact, most elderly people continue to look for, and find, help from their relatives. Only 5 percent of elderly people are cared for in nursing homes. In many families a tradition of mutual help and sharing is passed from one generation to the next. Parents love and care for their children, both help each other in adulthood, and then as parents reach old age, more of the caring shifts to the younger generation. Feelings of love and compassion continue to be the basis of many relationships providing support to the older people and satisfaction to the younger ones.

As your parents require more help, roles shift in a significant way. Chances are, for the first time in the history of your relationship, you are giving more help to your parents than you receive from them. This is sometimes called role reversal. It is a somewhat misleading and even dangerous phrase, because it implies that children become parents to their parents. This is never true. To act as if it were so is to run the risk of patronizing older people. What is true is that as your parents become frail, they may require help meeting their own needs as young children also require help. In old age many lose the ability to drive a car, manage their money, even wash, toilet, and feed themselves, and you may have to fill the gaps. At some level even the most diminished old people are aware of their loss and find it uncomfortable, or even embarrassing, that they need help. You can minimize their discomfort and dignify the care you give when you are sensitive to your parents' present need but also their former competence.

Taking on new responsibilities comes at some cost — a cost that many willingly accept, but one that has to be paid in any case. Willing or not, you will sometimes feel inadequate to the task of caring for your parents. At times you will despair of finding the necessary patience, time, energy, and tolerance. Martha was surprised when she became impatient with her mother. She assumed they would adjust easily to living together, but on some days she thought she could not tolerate another evening of trying to find time to help her son with his homework or another morning of her mother's painstaking efforts to dress herself. This is entirely normal.

Most of us can call up new reserves for a limited period, but your parents' frailty may outlast your supplies. You may need to use the resources of others — a professional, family, or friend — when yours are inadequate. Also, it's worth remembering that your parents do not need you to be perfect. They can probably understand if you are occasionally overwhelmed and ill-tempered, especially if you explain how you are feeling and have the grace to apologize when appropriate.

Am I Up to This?

Pat was surprised to hear herself say "scared." She was normally too shy to speak in groups, but she was shaken out of her usual reserve by the image of her mother needing even more of her help.

It scares me to hear about your situation, Martha. My mother is just beginning to decline and already I'm not sure I can take on more.

My Mom is still living on her own — just — but for the past year I've needed to check on her every day. The signs of slippage are everywhere. She used to be a fussy housekeeper, but now she doesn't seem to notice the dust, and I even find moldy food in the fridge. I know its unimportant in the scale of things, but I get really upset that she doesn't change her clothes. If I let her, she would wear the same thing every day, dirty or not.

I've always been close to my mom too. We were best friends really. My brother and sister are another story, though. They make me mad. They dutifully phone Mom each week but never try to find out how she's really doing. "What we don't know won't worry us" seems to be their motto. But I see Mom every day and can't pretend she isn't deteriorating. And I'm afraid I won't be able to manage.

Most of you are very busy — with jobs, children, spouses, and, often, community work. When caring for elderly relatives is added to such a load, it is not surprising that you may feel you have stepped over the line from being busy to being overwhelmed. Providing care for parents does not take the place of other duties. It is added on as an extra that has to be squeezed out of a limited number of hours in the day. The demands fall particularly heavily on women, who are the traditional caregivers.

One of the most significant recent changes in our society is the tremendous increase in the number of women who work outside the home. It is a shift that has repercussions for the elderly and those who care for them. It is not that adult children care less about their parents than children did in the past but, in many ways, it is more difficult to provide what they need. Care takes time and time is in short supply for many people. Most women do not have the option of giving up their job. They may be single or, like Pat, their family needs the second income.

As adult children move from young adulthood to middle age their responsibilities change, but they do not lessen. They often take on multiple roles in their jobs and in the community. Nor are their duties toward their own children over. Teenagers, for instance, do not need the constant supervision that younger children require, but few parents of adolescents consider that they have moved into a less challenging or less stressful stage of parenting. They are called on to be chauffeurs, confidantes, police, and, frequently, scapegoats. Many stay closely involved with their children as they in turn reach adulthood and become parents themselves.

Whatever your particular situation, care of an elderly parent is an added responsibility for which time and space must somehow be made. Someone has to help, and that someone is you. No wonder you are panicked and afraid: panicked because you have no choice, afraid you may not measure up to the task or that the demand may exceed your tolerance and stamina.

Facing Diminishment

Laura was fighting back tears.

> *I just can't get my father out of my mind. He has changed so much since I visited him at Christmas. I thought then that something was wrong. He wasn't on top of things as he usually is — he kept asking me how many people were there for dinner, for instance —*

but I put it down to the confusion of having four extra people in his house, two of them very active little kids. My mom didn't seem concerned, so I didn't give it much thought after I left.

But I should have worried. My parents have just been here for a vacation, and it's clear something is very wrong. Dad's memory is terrible. A dozen times a day he asked my mom when they were going home. He couldn't even keep the children's names straight.

I haven't seen much of my parents since I left high school — I was busy, they were busy — but it never occurred to me that they wouldn't always be there. Of course, they'd die sometime, but they're not even old. I feel I'm losing my father. He used to be so interested in everything we did, even ask about our friends, but now he can't always follow a conversation.

I finally took my mom aside and asked what was going on. She'd gone with him to their doctor, who evidently thought he had some kind of dementia, probably Alzheimer's disease. He'll have a brain scan when they return home. The doctor said something about him continuing to get more confused and eventually being too much for my mother to care for.

I feel as if I'm in the midst of a bad dream. One thought that keeps coming back is that my kids won't know their real grandfather. He was a fun grandad, always creating some interesting project. That part of him has disappeared already.

Whether your parents are emotionally close or distant, live near or far, whether they are old or young, sick or well, they probably occupy a special place inside you. When they leave, a gap is left. Sometimes heart attacks, strokes, or a number of other physical conditions change people's lives with numbing speed. Sometimes, as for Laura, a dementing illness leaves the body intact but changes the person you know. However they are robbed of their essence, you lose something of importance.

A sense of loss can come gradually, as for Laura's mother, who seemed to barely notice the gradual changes in her husband. For Laura, who rarely saw her father, the same deterioration appeared to be dramatic and without warning.

It is not unusual for children like Laura to be caught by surprise by the apparently sudden deterioration in their parents' health. Children and parents are taken up with their own lives, and though each knows that the older people's independence may not last forever, each acts as if it will. We rarely plan for something that may not happen.

Parents often conceal their difficulties, especially from their children. Men, in particular, are sometimes reluctant to talk to others about problems they or their wives are experiencing. As a consequence, adult children may be shocked on seeing a situation they did not even know existed. Laura's mother delayed talking to her about her father's illness because she did not want to upset her, telling herself that Laura was busy with her own family and did not need another person to worry about. But delay does not lessen the pain of loss that comes when you realize your parent is failing. Grief is an integral aspect of loving.

In the midst of a crisis it is often difficult to grieve. Practical problems are compelling, especially if they need immediate attention. And they are easier to concentrate on than sadness. By avoiding the pain, we feel more in control. Laura, for instance, was caught in a confusion of questions. Should her parents move close to her? How would her mother manage? How could she help her? There were many more questions than answers. These considerations do not leave much room for loss and grief. Such feelings are pushed underground where they do not disappear but wait to surface at unexpected times.

Coping with Anger

Donna felt uncomfortable. She suspected she was in a different position from anyone else in the group.

> You all seem to care about your parents. I'm not sure I do. I don't want to have to help my mother. I feel I've been doing that all my life, and I'm fed up with it.
>
> I did get a phone call about my mother. It was from my aunt, who lives near her. What my aunt said was that I needed to do something—and soon. My mother is about to lose her apartment because the landlord is fed up with complaints from the neighbors about her loud radio and constant requests for help with transportation, lost clothing, or money. I suppose she shouldn't really be living alone anyway because her eyesight is pretty bad.
>
> But why is it me who has to solve the problem? Just because I'm her daughter? I moved away years ago just so that I could have a life of my own, and here I am caught again. The trouble is that my mother doesn't have anyone else. I was mad at my aunt when she dumped this on my lap but, to be honest, she does the best she can and she's not well herself. I'm an only child and

my father has never been in the picture. My mother isn't exactly your maternal type. I don't remember her cooking a proper meal or coming to any event at my school. In fact, I looked after her most of the time. Like, coming home from school and finding her passed out on the floor after a drinking binge. She hasn't drunk much recently — I give her credit for that — but otherwise she hasn't changed. She still doesn't take responsibility for much, leaving bills unpaid, messes for other people to clear up. I guess I'm the one who has to deal with this mess.

Anger is a feeling that is so uncomfortable for most of us that we try to ignore it. Encouraged from childhood to be pleasing and accommodating, we try to dismiss any feelings of anger we experience: "I shouldn't feel that way." "What's the point?" "It does more harm than good." In our culture there are such strong social pressures against women expressing anger that they often have difficulty even identifying that it is anger that they feel. Yet, anger is a normal human response. In itself, it is neither right nor wrong. What we do as a result of our feeling is the part to be concerned with.

When your parents need help, you may feel angry for many reasons: the demands on you are already too many; you resent that your siblings are not doing their share; like Donna, you feel trapped by a parent for whom you feel little affection. Whatever its source, the anger deserves attention because it is a certain indication that something is amiss.

Denial does not make anger disappear. Repressed anger only creates problems, often emerging as anxiety, pessimism, and depression. If you fail to recognize that you feel used, unappreciated, or unfairly burdened, you may feel helpless and badly about yourself instead. Under a barrage of self-criticism, your legitimate needs are changed into feelings of inadequacy and incompetence — self-defeating feelings that are not helpful to anyone.

In a reverse process, you may turn anger not inward, but outward. You feel unlucky, unfairly treated, resentful that your parents need your help. Occasionally, you displace your feelings on to some other person, or aim them at the proverbial cat. In close relationships, feelings such as anger and frustration are often dumped on the wrong person. Arriving home tired from work and from a trying visit with an elderly parent, you may easily find undeserved fault with your own children. At the extreme, displaced feelings turn into scapegoating, where one person, usually weak and vulnerable, becomes the habitual victim of the other's stress. Everyone suffers when anger is ignored or when it is acted out rather than responded to as a sign that something is wrong.

Like all emotions, anger appears unbidden and is often intense, but you do have a choice about how you handle it. Once recognized, it is less likely to be damaging and may even lead to constructive change. The next step is to identify the cause and do something about that. Venting, blaming, and complaining may be helpful in the short run but rarely solve the problem. Better to address the root, whether that means asking for help, taking time for yourself, limiting how much you do, or talking to someone outside the situation to help you see it more clearly.

Obviously, not all problems can be easily alleviated. Sometimes you are stuck with a situation that makes you angry but about which you can do nothing. Your siblings may refuse to do their share. Your parents may need much help and little is available. Under these circumstances, you will probably continue to feel uncomfortable but at least your anger is focused on the appropriate target — whether it is lack of services, irresponsible relatives, or an unkind fate — instead of floating free, ready to attach itself to where it does not belong. Recognized and named, anger does not have to spoil relationships or destroy your peace of mind.

The Tyranny of Guilt

Susie was one of several people in the room who called out "guilt" as her reaction to my fictional scene.

I'd feel so bad if a neighbor noticed there was something wrong with my mother before I did. I see my mom every day, just to see that she's okay, so I'd certainly know if she were in trouble. Though I must say, despite the time I spend with her, she isn't doing well. Physically she's fine, but she's so lonely.

When my dad died, Mom and I decided she should live near me. We've always gotten along well. This way we would see more of each other and I could keep an eye on her. That was six months ago. It hasn't worked out the way I hoped. I thought she'd make friends and find things to do with people of her own age but that hasn't happened. I think she just waits for my visits and between times thinks of reasons to phone me, usually wanting help with some chore, such as adjusting the thermostat, which she could normally do herself. I find myself thinking about her a lot while I'm at work, which doesn't help my concentration.

I picture her alone in her apartment, with nothing to do except watch the television. There must be something I can do to make her happier.

"Guilt" is a word that comes up frequently in conversations about elderly parents. It is another of those unpleasant feelings that tells us we are to blame for something. We are doing something, or failing to do something for which we will be criticized, either by others or by our own conscience. Invariably, we are our own most severe critics.

Appropriate guilt is part of the glue that holds society together. If we did not learn that stealing, cheating, and violence are wrong and may be punished, our world would be even more crime-ridden and brutal than it is. So, feelings of guilt about a parent may be a sign that we are not acting in a caring or considerate way. Like all feelings, this is worth taking time to understand. It helps to ask the question "Given the circumstances, am I acting as responsibly as I am able?"

There is another type of guilt, however, that is self-inflicted and tyrannical. Some call this "false" guilt. It is best described as a sense that we personally can, and should, do something about any problem in our parents' lives. If only we try hard enough, our parents will be less lonely, less bored, enjoy life more. False guilt creates impossible demands. No matter how much we do, it is never good enough.

Women are particularly prone to taking on responsibility for others' happiness. Many women feel that it is up to them to ensure that the rest of the family enjoys the vacation or Christmas, for example, and that guests have a good visit. There is some truth in the belief that effort can make a difference. If Susie were to visit her mother in the evenings as well as the mornings, and spend several hours with her, her mother would probably be less lonely and somewhat happier, at least while they were together. Susie has to balance all parts of her life, however, and she can solve her mother's problem only by sacrificing the needs of her children, her husband, and herself. By acting as if she is responsible for her mother's loneliness, she is taking on a responsibility that is not hers but her mother's. This is "false" guilt at work.

Most adult children act as lovingly as they are able, but they may unwittingly put themselves in a no-win situation. Feelings of guilt bear no relation to how much one cares. Many people do a great deal for their parents — travel long distances, visit frequently, run errands, do chores — but still berate themselves for not doing enough. One woman I know finally recognized that she was doing as much as she could for her mother but then felt badly because she was not always doing it with a song in her heart. She could not win.

Some parents are expert at inducing guilt. They may drop comments such as "I know how busy you are," or "Don't bother about me. All I want is for you to have a good time." Guilt finds a ready home in the hearts of most adult children, but ultimately it is something you can choose to accept or reject. It helps if you are clear about your expectations of yourself. How often are you prepared to visit? Are you available to transport? How much notice do you need? In short, given the circumstances — your own, your parents' — what are you able realistically to take on?

Like Susie, you need to assess what you can do and are prepared to do for your parents. To ask "What should I do?" or "What ought I to do?" is rarely useful. "Should" and "ought" carry unrealistic standards. Whenever you think or speak those words it is worth looking at the feelings or beliefs that lie behind them. It may then be possible to decide how much power to give them. For instance, many people carry a standard that because their parents cared for them, they should do as much in return. What about this "should"? Children sign no contract with their parents. Because children do not ask to be born, they have a right to be cared for with no obligation to repay. They in turn do the same as parents to their own children. Most adult children want to be loving and caring to their parents and often go to considerable effort to do so, but, for the most part, there is a limit to their sacrifice, and it falls short of the time, money, and effort their parents spent on raising them.

Unexamined, the "shoulds" and "oughts" generate a feeling that you have fallen short, that you are inadequate or unloving. Difficult though the task is, it is far more useful to assess your circumstances, your parents' needs, the feelings you have for each other, and then decide what is possible.

Pervasive Sadness

Connie looked at her husband, John, before she offered her reaction: "sadness."

I'm thinking about John's father and how sad it would be for us if he suddenly became sick or disabled. It's strange that he's the person who comes to mind because we came here to learn how to help John's mother. She has Parkinson's disease and lives in a nursing home. It's so difficult to visit her there. Sometimes she's so confused she doesn't know who we are her, but at other times she's fairly clear and asks us when she can go home because she doesn't like where she is. I don't know which is worse. It's so sad. Why do people have to linger on like this? John finds it so awful that he can rarely bring himself to visit. I understand how he feels but I also think about how I'd feel if my kids didn't come to see me. And it will be our turn one day.

John's father is a wonderful man. He cared for his wife for years even after she needed help with dressing and going to the bathroom. But it finally got to be too much for him and he had to find a nursing home for her. We hoped he'd get some rest and have some fun. He does look much better but his main occupation is visiting his wife. He misses her so much that he spends almost as much time with her now as when she was living at home. John has only been able to persuade him to play one game of golf, and when he comes to us for a meal, he leaves almost as soon as he has eaten to return to the nursing home. He's like a lost soul.

It is sad to see our parents develop health problems, lose people close to them, and have to restrict their activities. The sadness is accompanied by pain if they are suffering or have lost the wish to live. Old age is a harsh time for some parents, and, however hard we try, we may be able to do little to make it better. It is sometimes difficult to make sense of a world that lets people linger on in pain, whether emotional or physical, long past the point when they would have chosen to die.

As our parents grow frail, we feel for them and also for ourselves. It is no longer possible to hide from the fact that we will soon live in a world without them. In our culture, many of us reach middle age with little personal experience of death. Death of parents in their old age may be the first time we have lost someone very close.

Under this sadness is another layer. Here we face the prospect of our own old age and death. Our parents' decline brings us face to face with our own mortality. Relatives in the generation above act as a buffer protecting us from our decline, which appears on a distant horizon while our parents are still vigorous. When they begin to fail, however, we are forced to face the reality that we are next in line. We find ourselves thinking more about our own old age, what will it be like and how we will handle it.

Deferred Dreams

Debbie didn't say anything at first. When she did speak, she sounded bitter.

> *I'm here because it looks as if I'm going to be stuck with my mother, and I'm resenting it. But she can't be on her own any longer, and I'm the only one of my brothers and sisters who has the room and doesn't work. By rights, it should be my sister caring for her — she was Mom's favorite — but she's divorced and works all day. So, even though Mom and I were never close, it's good old me that will save everyone again.*
>
> *It seems to me that I've been looking after people all my life. First my kids — we have five — and then my father-in-law, who lives next door. He's one of those helpless men around the house, so I've been taking meals in to him since his wife died. Now he can't drive so I take him shopping. It's not much bother really except when my husband and I think of going away. I retired last year and he's going to in June. We thought we'd buy a small camper so that we could travel. For the first time in our lives we have money and time to please ourselves. It would be wonderful to take off, just the two of us, with no time limit and no one else to think about.*
>
> *Now it looks as if we'll have Mum. Another dream melted away. I never thought it would be our parents who'd stop us enjoying our retirement. It seems unfair. Will it ever be my turn to do what I want?*

The added responsibility of frail parents never comes at a convenient time. Usually you are too busy building a home and family or making a living to have resources to spare. Nor does freedom from those responsibilities necessarily make it easier for you to care for your parents. Retirement brings its own set of circumstances. Many couples have dreams and plans that involve travel or even a move to another area. Just as you are hoping to cast off responsibilities and obligations that have tied you to one place, your parents need your care. You may be responsible for more than one, two, or even three elderly relatives who have no one else to look out for them. Like Debbie, you may feel that much of your life has been dominated by taking care of others, first your children, then parents and in-laws. Add to that possible problems with your own health or that of your spouse. Over the age of sixty, a large proportion of people have medical conditions that require regular treatment. Of these a significant number find their health is quite impaired and they have no time or energy to give to others.

The decline of your parents is one of those unfortunate occurrences that you deplore, but cannot ignore. "Why is this happening to me?" "Why now?" It feels unfair that you are so unlucky. You may even resent your parents for being the unwitting creators of the trap in which you find yourself. If your parents are difficult, ungrateful, or in a situation they could have prevented by thought and planning, your resentment probably mounts.

Understandable though resentment is, it can be destructive to everyone, especially the one who feels it most. Like other negative feelings, it can poison relationships unless you find a way of dealing with it. It colors everything you do, eroding any sense of satisfaction or achievement you might otherwise gain from helping your parents when they need it. Perhaps you can discover what is behind your feeling. What do you need that you are not getting? Help? Appreciation? Time to yourself? The situation is unfortunate but it exists and you have to deal with it somehow. With honest soul-searching, the way you choose can minimize the negative repercussions.

Points to Consider

1. You will experience a wide range of feelings as your parents grow old. Recognize what you are feeling.

2. Feelings exist whether you like them or not. Facing them and learning about them helps you control what you do about them.

3. Your involvement with your parents is likely to be more positive and satisfactory if you are clear about what you can and are prepared to do, rather than being driven by guilt and what you think you *should* do.

4. Caring for elderly parents is often a stress and a burden but with thought and some effort it may also be a source of satisfaction.

5. No one says it will be easy.

· *Chapter 2* ·

Landmarks of Aging:
What Your Parents Face

❧

IN OLDER YEARS, age itself has little meaning. To say that a man is seventy-five years old is not to say much except that he is male and has been alive for three-quarters of a century. It tells nothing about his health, his relationships, his interests, his sense of himself. It does not say whether he can walk, drive a car, or carry on a coherent conversation. By contrast, the beginning of life is well-charted terrain with reasonably predictable milestones indicating when children begin to crawl, walk, and talk. But the older we grow, the less age alone can tell much of any substance about a person.

Thinking about your parents as they adjust to the changes that come with old age, it is *their* needs, not those of the elderly as a group, that are important. There are no clear landmarks. Their old age starts when they are no longer able to do what they have always been able to do, and it becomes significant as they lose the ability to manage without help.

Old age may cover many years. It is commonly thought to start with retirement and, certainly, ends with death. For most people, this means a period of eleven to twenty-five years — not an insignificant span. Such a large number of people, with ages ranging from early sixties to late nineties, cannot be treated as a homogeneous group. Indeed, someone who is old is probably more unlike his or her peers than at any other time of life. Look at a group of adolescents and it is clear that as individuals they have not yet fully developed their own distinctness of being. Much of their social energy goes into comparing themselves with their peers and striving not to be too different. Over the next decades they will accumulate experiences — successes, disappointments, joys, and sadnesses — that will shape the people they will become in old age. It is not only experiences that change us but also the way we choose to deal with them. Each of us develops a particular way of dealing with the ups and downs life. Some are optimistic, some expect life to be difficult, some fight perceived injustices, some adapt. By old age, styles are well entrenched. One woman in her eighties told me, "As I grow older, I only become more so!"

There are, however, some generalizations and a few milestones in old age that are worth noting. Most sixty-five-year-olds have very different issues of health, needs, and concerns from people twenty years older. For purposes of discussion, if not elegance, gerontologists usually divide the elderly into young-old, old-old, and even mid-old. Before their mid-seventies, most people need no help in managing their lives; they are as independent as they have ever been. In fact, most people of this age give more help to the members of their family than they receive. Beyond that time, however, there is an increased likelihood that they will need some assistance.

One predictable change is physical. When people over the age of sixty write or talk about themselves, they frequently make the point that they do not feel their age. In the mirror, their external wrinkles and gray hair remind them, often with a rude shock, that they are old. Inside they feel much younger. Inevitably, however, body and mind begin to send unmistakable messages that time takes a toll. It takes longer to recover from an attack of the flu. The inability to remember names becomes not just inconvenient but embarrassing. Such signs become more frequent and more distressing. While no one enjoys such changes, most people adjust to them without having to alter their lives significantly.

The risk of serious ill health, however, also increases with advancing years. Problems may come suddenly, as with stroke, or slowly, as with dementia. In either case, health problems lead to a life dramatically different.

It is ironic that the elderly are frequently stereotyped as inflexible and unable to face new challenges. In reality, people probably have to deal with more new situations in the last years of their lives than at any time since adolescence.

Other changes are emotional or social. Poor health, relocation, and the death of relatives and friends are the most common. Some changes, like retirement, may be a cause for celebration. Others, such as the loss of a spouse, are traumatic. All changes create a shift that requires adjustment. In old age, the challenges may come fast and often. I worked with a man who, in the span of just one year, saw his wife of fifty-two years die of a heart attack, lost his brother to cancer, had his own leg amputated due to complications from diabetes, was confined to a wheelchair, and ended up living with his son. Often, as for that man, one change precipitates another. Poor health alters living arrangements, deteriorating eyesight removes ability to drive, deafness effects social life. Most of my elderly clients find old age difficult to take at times. Your parents probably do too. "Old age is not for sissies" is an oft-echoed refrain.

Not all is loss, however. Many people describe aspects of their old age as very satisfying. With more time and fewer obligations, many find opportunities for new activities and wider interests. My father, for example, found that he felt healthier physically and mentally after he retired; he was able to alternate exercise, rest, eating, and work according to his inclinations and needs. Free of the schedule of his workplace, he could choose when and how he was busy.

Relationships become increasingly important and may deepen with age as parents have more contact with their friends, siblings, and especially children. When asked to whom they turn for help, whom they confide in, think and talk about, most elderly parents put their children first. It is with their children that older people hope to give and receive most of their love and support.

As you become more involved with your aging parents, the ways in which they handle the changes they face will have an impact on your life too.

Retirement

Mr. and Mrs. Casey anticipated their retirement with pleasure. They talked about all the things that they would be able to do. They did not think of themselves as entering old age, and treated their eligibility for "Golden Age discounts" as something of a joke. What they looked forward to was the freedom to do what they wanted to do, unhampered by the demands of their jobs.

For the last year of his work, Mr. Casey found himself quite drained. By the time he got home, he had interest for little except the newspaper and television, in front of which he invariably fell asleep. He retired in January. The plan was for Mrs. Casey to stay at her job for another year. It seemed a sensible arrangement. She worked part-time so was home by early afternoon, and the money was useful.

For Mr. Casey, the first few weeks of his retirement were strangely disorienting. He was not used to being in the house alone. It was amazing how slowly time passed. He found chores to do, but noticed himself watching the clock for his wife's return.

Over the next months, he did develop a routine that helped him feel more productive. He had to admit, though, that the long-anticipated freedom from work was not as pleasurable as he thought it would be. Sometimes he was bored. Perhaps his wife should retire, and then they could have some fun together.

For her part, Mrs. Casey was not entirely happy being at the office while her husband was home. It was an odd feeling for her too. For the first time in their marriage, Mr. Casey was at home alone and doing some of the cleaning and cooking. Mrs. Casey joked to her friends about this new and wonderful arrangement, but in reality she wanted to be back in charge of her own house. And her job interfered with their time together. After six months, when she decided that she would retire also, her husband was delighted.

Like the Caseys, your parents have probably looked forward to retirement. Most people do. Retirement is looked to as a time for some rest and relaxation or as an opportunity for travel, hobbies, a new career.

Some people, however, dread the end of their working life. Those whose chief interest and purpose in life is bound up with their job are likely to have a difficult time when they no longer have one to go to. They feel unproductive and unimportant. They find themselves with too much leisure and too few interests to make that time fulfilling. Another group for whom retirement may be difficult are single people who live alone. They may find themselves isolated and lonely if work was also the primary focus of their social activity.

Whether they regard retirement with pleasure or apprehension, your parents will go through a period of adjustment when the time comes for them to stop work. Surprisingly few retirees plan for this stage of their lives except to look at their finances. Income is undeniably an important consideration, but adjustment is a much broader task. It will take time and deliberation to create new routines, new interests and activities. Those who think about such matters before their jobs end can ease the transition for themselves and do much to make retirement as pleasurable as they hoped.

As people think about retirement they often talk about those activities for which they never had time: "When I retire I'll try rock climbing"; "I've always thought I'd paint." The activities and interests your parents pursue after they have retired are likely to be similar to those they pursued when younger. There is great satisfaction in improving their skills or developing them more fully.

Your parents may choose to return to paid employment, partly for financial reasons but partly because they find it satisfying to continue to feel useful. Or they may become volunteers, working in an area that holds some appeal for them. Any activity that nourishes a sense of continuing competence is worth encouraging.

In general, your mother will adjust to retirement more easily than your father. For many older women, paid employment has not been a dominant feature of their lives. Even if they have worked outside the home, much of their daily routine is not affected by ceasing that job. Cooking, cleaning, and shopping continue and provide a structure for the day. Many of their friendships, with neighbors, with family, are not ruptured by leaving the workplace. Indeed, important relationships may deepen as there is more time to spend together.

For your parents as a couple, more time together may be a plus or a minus. One thing is certain: retirement will affect their relationship. We will touch on this again later in this chapter.

Grandparenting

One of the pleasures of retirement for Mrs. Casey was the chance to see more of her family. Her daughter lived in the same town, but when they were both working, there had been little time to get together and few opportunities to be with her grandchildren. Now, each Tuesday, Mr. and Mrs. Casey fetched their two grandchildren from school and cared for them until their daughter came home.

Mr. Casey had been lukewarm at first when his wife suggested this arrangement but to his surprise found himself looking forward to the days with the grandchildren. It was fun to have his grandson help him. He planned chores that they could do together. Similarly, Mrs. Casey enjoyed having small children around again. She found she had more patience teaching her granddaughter to knit than she had had for her own children. Of course, in those days, there had been so much else she had to do. Also, she had to admit, it was easier to be patient when she knew that the children would be leaving in two hours. She also delighted in the fact that when her daughter fetched the children, the two of them had time for a chat and a cup of tea together.

Grandparents come in different models, many of which do not fit the stereotype of the nurturing, stay-at-home "grandmom and granddad" that the Caseys illustrate. As young adults, you probably expect your parents not only to love your children, but also to feel privileged to spend time with them and even to care for them on occasion. You may be mistaken. Your parents may be so busy with their own activities that they are rarely home. Some do want to spend a great deal of time with their grandchildren, whereas others want a break from the caregiving that they feel they have been doing all their lives. Some love to read or play with young children while you are nearby but do not want the responsibility of being in sole charge. As their health deteriorates, your parents may find the noise and commotion of your children exhausting, or find some ages impossible. They might prefer short, frequent visits, and especially enjoy seeing one child at a time.

A friend of mine described her feelings about the different ages of her grandchildren. "Babies, of course, are adorable and elicit the most hugging. Toddlers are cute and funny, but too exhausting for many of us to cope with. The grade school years may be the most satisfying. The kids can still be hugged a little, like to do things together, still love cookies, and still respond. We are locked in the closet for most of the teen years unless we are visitors from afar, bearing gifts. In that case, we get a hasty hug on their way by and out."

When your children and your parents can get to know each other, it is often a special relationship for both generations. Free of the responsibility of being *the* parent, many older people report that they can relax and enjoy their grandchildren more than they could their own children. For your part, you may see a softer, more tolerant side of your parents. In happy circumstances, your mutual interest and love for the children will bring you and your parents emotionally closer.

Marriage

For the Caseys, the days quickly fell into a comfortable routine. Mrs. Casey took back total responsibility for the housekeeping, while Mr. Casey worked on the car and garden. They enjoyed knowing that the other was around. If they wanted to go out for the day, they could just get up and go. Mrs. Casey felt that she had never had so few worries. They had enough money, they both were healthy, and their children were doing well. Life was more relaxed than it had ever been.

If there was any problem with retirement for Mrs. Casey, it was that she had too little time alone. She loved her husband dearly, but he was always around. She was delighted when he joined a men's bowling league. The experiment was a success. Both enjoyed their time apart and happily exchanged news when they were back together.

Old age is a stable period for most marriages. Your parents have probably found a way of being with each other that is, for the most part, comfortable and satisfying. With more time to spend together, with fewer responsibilities, with more need to care for and nurture each other, many couples find their relationship more intimate and companionable than ever before.

If your parents have a difficult relationship, they may have reached some level of acceptance of their differences and discontent. Watching their dissatisfaction, you may find it hard to understand why they stay together. But divorce among the elderly is far less common than at younger ages. The familiar brings a certain security and comfort that are preferable to the unknown.

Stable relationships are not necessarily static, however. Changes do occur. In all marriages, whatever happens to one partner also affects the other, and both have to adjust. Two events that are almost certain to alter the relationship are retirement and chronic poor health.

Though your parents may have spent several decades together, retirement may be the first time they have spent all day and every day in each other's company. Such togetherness may be more than the relationship can easily stand: "I married him for better or worse but not for lunch." No two people can meet all of each other's needs, but they may not realize that until the absence of work and children make it evident. When leisure was limited, they may have chosen to spend that time together. After retirement, however, when most of the day is made up of discretionary time, one or both partners eventually find that there is such a thing as too much companionship. Each person's needs are different. One enjoys going shopping alone occasionally, another loves having the house to herself for a while, another likes to meet a friend without being part of a couple each time. How to balance "time alone" with "time together" can be a delicate challenge for couples to negotiate.

Similarly, if one of your parents becomes disabled, the relationship is then profoundly changed. Your healthier parent has to assume more care and responsibility for tasks for which he or she may have little skill, limited energy, or no liking. Both parents may find activities closed to them as life becomes restricted to the capacity of the least able partner. If one is not able to handle a visit to a neighbor for supper, both stay home; if one cannot sit for long periods in the car, neither goes on trips. Togetherness in this case is thrust upon them by need, not by choice.

Sometimes called the "hidden victim," your caregiving parent probably experiences signs of stress. This is particularly true if your sick parent has a dementing illness, which changes his or her personality and behavior. The caregiver has to provide supervision and care to a partner who no longer bears much resemblance to the person he or she married. However great the commitment and abiding affection, it is a rare person who does not find this situation trying and painful. And for couples who did not have a good relationship when they were well, a debilitating dementia is close to intolerable.

Sickness and Disability

Poor health brought a dramatic change in Mr. and Mrs. Casey's lives. There had been minor alarms, such as Mrs. Casey's high blood pressure, but none serious enough to slow them down. Then, ten years after he retired, Mr. Casey had a heart attack. He made a good recovery according to his cardiologist, but he was never to feel really well again. He was constantly aware that he had less stamina than he used to have and had pain in his chest if he exerted himself much.

The emotional change was as evident as the physical. He became very concerned about his body, monitoring every sign for possible trouble. Mrs. Casey was just as watchful. For both, his health became a preoccupation.

Slowly but surely, the couple's lives became circumscribed by Mr. Casey's condition. They stopped going on trips, anxious about being far from their doctor and hospital. At home, their routine became more rigid as Mr. Casey was less able to handle the commotion of visitors or the absence of regular rest periods.

Mrs. Casey rarely went out because her husband became so anxious without her. And the grandchildren did not visit much now. She realized that the circle of their lives was narrowing, bound by his illness. Inexorably, he became an invalid.

Physical health cannot be looked at in isolation. Mind and body are intricately intertwined. The way people react to illness and disability cannot be separated from their personality, social situation, or interests. Even something as concrete as the ability to move around the house has differing repercussions depending on whether your parent lives alone, puts a high value on being active, or is willing to accept help. I was struck by this difference when, within one week, I saw two women experiencing problems with their eyesight. One became depressed and discouraged when she was no longer able to do the fine embroidery that meant so much to her. The other's eyesight was actually worse, but she could still watch television and do things that were important to her. She came to see me, not about herself, but because she was concerned about her daughter's marriage. One person's disability is another's inconvenience.

A stereotype of the elderly is that they talk about little except their aches and pains. Doctors and nurses report, however, that most of their older patients downplay difficulties and pay them too little attention. Many older people brush concerns aside, assuming they are inevitable and untreatable aspects of growing old. In contrast, others find poor health frightening and spend much time checking how their bodies are working. They can become preoccupied with real or imaginary symptoms, suffering from an anxiety that feeds on itself and has the unfortunate side effect of alienating those nearby.

Sickness is one way of getting attention. It is tragedy that for many old people, poor health is one of the few acceptable ways of doing so. People whose world has become limited to their own four walls, who see only the occasional visitor and can no longer follow the news or television, have very little to talk about. The state of their health may be the most available subject of conversation. And perhaps it will elicit some interest. Nurses who treat the sick in their own homes often find themselves in a dilemma. Lonely patients may not put much work into getting well because their efforts to improve mean the loss of the nurse's enjoyable visits.

Illness and disability do not have to be life-threatening to be isolating. Most pernicious are the chronic conditions that make it very difficult for people to leave the house or take any interest in the world. Deafness, poor eyesight, and crippling arthritis can effectively cut people off from others. And, for old people, the world does not always come to them. Many of their friends also find it difficult to get around. Nor do people have to live alone to be lonely. Couples in which one partner is disabled sometimes find that friends assume that because they "have each other" they do not need other company. Those whose partner is disabled by a dementia are in a particularly painful position, caught in a social no-man's land without the freedom to form another relationship.

Sex

Sexuality in the elderly is widely ignored. Many young people are surprised and even shocked to hear that men and women in their seventies and eighties are attracted to each other, have sexual feelings, and even act on them. Yet many elderly people report that they are not only sexually active but enjoy it as much as they have ever done.

But problems can and do occur. Brought up in an age when bodies were not discussed, older people are often reluctant to seek help or ask questions. Men may feel embarrassed to talk about their sexual difficulties and women may feel ashamed that they have sexual desires. It is not uncommon for my older single women clients to mention their frustration and sadness that they no longer enjoy sexual intimacy with a partner. Invariably, they have never shared these feelings before, afraid that they may be revealing something unnatural or even depraved. They certainly sense that their children would be embarrassed.

Even doctors often fail to ask about the effect of illness and treatment on their older patients' sexual activity. Yet it is physical and mental illness and the medications used to treat them that are frequently the culprits affecting a person's ability to have and enjoy sexual intercourse. Misinformation is another culprit. Some couples may unnecessarily limit their lovemaking, for example, because they have heard that it will precipitate a heart attack.

Many people know little about how their bodies change sexually as they age, and that many conditions, such as vaginal dryness and difficulty in maintaining an erection, are a normal part of aging and can often be helped. Older people may be so embarrassed and afraid of failing that they withdraw from all physical affection, leaving their partner feeling unloved and unattractive. With openness and consideration, most couples can find satisfactory ways of being physically intimate.

People who are widowed or whose spouses are disabled are in a lonely situation sexually. What can they do? For single women, their longer life expectancy means that potential male partners are in short supply. For those whose spouses are sick, even in a nursing home, another sexual partner rarely seems an acceptable solution morally or socially. And masturbation, though more people are trying it (perhaps for the first time in their lives) and finding it pleasurable, is still widely regarded with shame.

Grief and Loss

Mr. Casey did not recover from his second heart attack. Before and during the funeral, Mrs. Casey moved around as if dazed. Looking back on that period later, she could remember very little. The most difficult time was after the funeral. For a few nights she stayed with her daughter, dreading her return home. Sleeping alone in their bed was a major hurdle, but she knew the longer she delayed, the higher the hurdle would become.

In practice, nights proved to be less of a challenge than the days. The house felt eerily empty. Supper time was the hardest. It was so lonely to eat on her own that there did not seem much point. Television served as a distraction, and she began snacking in the living room, mindlessly watching any program that happened to be on. She missed her husband horribly. They had been together almost fifty years and had always been good companions. Dozens of times a day, she found herself talking to him in her mind.

To relieve her loneliness, she found herself trying to think of reasons to call her daughter. Her daughter was considerate, calling or visiting at least twice a week. Mrs. Casey told herself that she could not expect more, but she had not realized how busy they all were. But in her bleakest moments she wished she'd died too.

Over the months, Mrs. Casey was able to pick up some of the threads of her old life. Activities she had dropped because of her husband's ill health were possible once again. She doubted that she would ever like living alone, but at least the pain of it abated. On good days, she even felt that there were some enjoyable aspects to being alone. She was much freer to do what she wanted to do. On bad days, there didn't seem much point in living.

Old age is sometimes called the season of loss. By the time they reach their eighties, your parents have certainly lost some vigor and physical resilience, friends and family will have died, and they may have had to move from their home and community, restrict their travel, and give up some activities.

The most devastating blow for your parents is, of course, the death of a spouse. Not only do they lose the companion with whom they have shared the majority of their lives, but also the person around whom the routine of their day, their social life, and even their identity have been built. The disruption is far-reaching and severe.

Everybody grieves in his or her own way. There is no right, or even best, way. Some are almost violent in their grief, others are silent, and some appear not to grieve at all. Some quickly adjust to a new life and put their sadness behind them, whereas others openly mourn their loss for the remainder of their lives. For still others, grief is a delayed process, with the deep sadness coming only months after the loved one has died.

Not only does each *person* experience loss in a different way, but each *loss* is experienced differently. So many things influence grief. The meaning of a particular death, whether death was sudden or expected, and the mourner's personality and previous experience with death are just a few of the factors that affect reactions.

During a consultation in a nursing home, the staff wanted to talk to me about a ninety-year-old woman whose eighty-four-year-old sister had just died. The two sisters had shared a room in the nursing home. The staff expressed some consternation that the older woman showed no sign of grief. Several of them were inclined to agree with her son that she had always been self-centered and her present behavior just confirmed that. My conversation with the old lady revealed something different. She was able to tell me that both she and her sister had been ready to die for some time, so she had no regrets that her sister now had her wish. Because they both had a strong religious faith, she knew without question that they would be together in the near future. For this woman there was little to mourn.

On another consultation, the nurses directed me to an elderly man who was depressed. On the surface it seemed that his depression had been triggered by the death of his cat. It was, in fact, a cumulative depression. During the past year, both his wife and sister had died. His emphysema had worsened to the point that he now required constant oxygen. He had apparently dealt with all these changes philosophically, without much conversation or complaint. The death of his cat was one loss too many. He was mourning, not only the loss of his animal, but the accumulated sorrows of the past year.

Some deaths are significant in ways that are difficult for others to recognize. A friend told me that her mother seemed more grief-stricken by the recent death of a close friend than she had been by the death of her husband, which had occurred twenty years previously. When my friend remarked on this, her mother agreed that she was more deeply affected by the loss of this particular woman than she expected. Her friend had been the one remaining close acquaintance who, like her, had grown up in Russia during the First World War and the tumultuous years of the Revolution. The two women often talked about their many shared memories. For my friend's mother, the death of her close friend inflicted not only the pain of lost companionship but also the loneliness of being a sole survivor.

Death can be the most devastating, but it is by no means the only deprivation in old age. Any change, however freely chosen, brings some loss along with it. For instance, your parents may decide to move to a retirement community. Their enthusiasm may be muted because they know they are planning for the day when they can no longer drive or fully care for themselves.

If asked to list their fears, your parents would probably put "being dependent on others" near the top. At all ages, help is more difficult to receive than give, from the toddler's "No, me do it myself" to the old person's "I don't want to be a burden to my children." Your parents may strive at all costs to retain the image of themselves as competent and in charge, even refusing help that they clearly need. You may admire their self-sufficiency,, but if they have a misplaced confidence in their competence, problems will inevitably arise. As your parents grow old, they have to evaluate and decide when a task that used to be routine is now not worth the risk; at some point the odds become great that consequences will be severe and seeking help shows good judgment. Illness and disability require people to deal with a new reality and accept that independence and competence may be defined in terms of using help appropriately. Learning to accept care with grace is one of the major challenges of old age.

Sense of Meaning

With their children grown, their spouse dead, and their activities restricted by poor health, some people feel that life has little meaning. Ours is a difficult society in which to grow old. We have become adept at lengthening the span of physical life, but we have lagged in our ability to give quality to that life. Most people experience their years beyond seventy as quite enjoyable and satisfying, but too many others find themselves feeling irrelevant and superfluous. They have a sense of marking time. Like all of us, old people want to feel that they have something to contribute and that they matter to someone.

During our lives we all play many different roles — child, sibling, student, spouse, parent, worker, colleague, friend. Indeed, it is in these terms that we often define ourselves. When asked to describe ourselves, most of us mention our jobs, our consuming interests, and our immediate family. For our parents, in their old age, many roles have either been curtailed or disappeared. In their absence, it is easy for people to feel that they have outlived their purpose.

One of the many wonderful paradoxes in life is that restriction in some areas leads to expansion in others. Relationships may deepen when work no longer takes so much time and energy; friends may become more important when children move away, and especially after spouses die; new activities may open up when retirement from paid work frees time; spiritual and emotional life may become richer as the future shortens. The dropping away of roles may bring on a feeling of uselessness and redundancy, but it may also lead to a sense of freedom — freedom from expectations, responsibilities, and convention. One woman found that her white hair and her cane helped her flout rules when crossing the street. She was sure that she was labeled as "senile," but she enjoyed a new sense of power when she stepped into the street and traffic stopped. Another woman appeared at the Senior Center with a new hairstyle and brighter, smarter clothes. She explained with some relish that her husband had considered hair and clothes frivolous items but now, as a widow, she had only herself to please. In one group I led, there was general agreement among the older women that they had more self-confidence and fewer inhibitions than when they were younger. As one member put it: "It's easier to take risks because I don't have much to lose at this point in my life."

In these and other ways, old age can be a period of personal growth and expansion. Personality development does not stop because one is old. The psychologist Erik Erikson was the first to write about adult development in a systematic way. He described life as a series of stages extending from birth until death, in each of which we have certain tasks to achieve. In the last two stages (from fifty years of age to death) he named the tasks "generativity" and "integrity." Generativity involves contributing to the world and passing on knowledge and wisdom to the younger generation. As they are parents to their adolescent children, mentors to young adults, guides to colleagues, people in their fifties and sixties provide examples and role models to those coming behind them. The final stage, that of integrity, is more inward-turning, as elderly people look back on their lives and find them a source of satisfaction. The hoped-for feeling is that despite some regrets and mistakes, they have a sense of pride and accomplishment, of a job well done. This, according to Erikson, is necessary before they can willingly let life go.

It is largely within the context of their families that your parents accomplish these tasks. It is there that they derive their sense of contributing to the world and their sense of continuity as you and your children live on after they have gone.

It is not only in this broad, existential framework that family is central. For your parents as they age, their family also gives them their deepest source of meaning on a daily basis. As their contemporaries die, as energy and mobility diminish, you may become even more important than formerly. You and your children become the focus of their interest and occupy much of their attention. Maybe more than you want. It can feel a burden to be so important. Parents are often nurtured by small signs of affection, however. Letters, telephone calls, short visits all can go a long way in expressing your sustained interest in your parents. Often the thoughtfulness of a gesture is more important than the gesture itself.

Parents of any age want to be proud of their children. With their parenting tasks behind them, it is especially important that they see themselves as having done a good job — as having provided their children with sound values, an education and skills necessary to succeed in the world. And they largely assess their achievement by how much attention their children give them. Your salary or your worldly importance can certainly give your parents pleasure, but they pale into insignificance compared with the affection you show. Their assessment of their accomplishments, their value, and even their self-esteem is much influenced by their relationships within the family.

Points to Consider

1. Your parents' health, contentment, and ability to be independent cannot be assessed solely on the basis of their age. Old people are very different from each other.

2. Don't assume that life is a downward slide for people just because they have reached their sixties. For many, old age is a satisfying and meaningful time of life, bringing more leisure, fewer responsibilities, new freedom.

3. Your parents may respond to their retirement with trepidation or pleasure. Either way, they will have a period of adjustment that might be difficult, especially if work has been an important part of their identity.

4. Older marriages are usually stable but not static. Retirement and poor health are just two of many changes that affect the relationship.

5. As your parents age, there are many changes. You will only know by listening to what they mean to your parent.

6. Grief is profound and often submerged. Your bereaved parent will probably still be grieving long after you think he or she should be "over it."

7. Along with other members of your family, you are probably very important to your parents. Your achievements, your struggles, and especially your attention give satisfaction, interest, and meaning to their lives.

· Chapter 3 ·

When to Act

❧

God, grant me the serenity to accept
The things I cannot change;
The courage to change the things I can,
And the wisdom to know the difference.

REINHOLD NIEBUHR'S well-used Serenity Prayer is a succinct and wise response to a question I am frequently asked by children concerned about their aging parents: "Should I be doing something I'm not?" On the face of it, it should be simple to distinguish what you can change from what you cannot, but when you think about people you love, the wisdom to know the difference becomes elusive. The facts may or may not be clear, and many emotions — both your parents' and your own — are certain to complicate your task. As you try to decide what, if any, action you should take, there are several questions that are helpful to bear in mind.

First of all, you have to ask if your parents need anything to be changed, and, if so, what is it. Many aspects of old age are distressing and, almost inevitably, your parents will have some hard times. But they may pass and require no dramatic action. Decide whether a problem exists before you try to solve it.

If you decide there is a problem, you then have to clarify who is troubled — you or your parents. Sometimes, your parents' situation is more painful for you than for them. Watching them deal with the challenges of growing old, you may need help yourself to deal with the feelings that arise.

After a careful appraisal, you will sometimes confirm that indeed something must be changed. If your parents can no longer manage alone, you have to step in to ensure that they are safe and as comfortable as possible. Along with asking what they need, consider how much you personally can do. To make a sound decision, you must give your own circumstances, as well as theirs, sufficient weight.

Unfortunately, grief and unhappiness are unavoidable in life, perhaps particularly in old age. Often there is no remedy. With love and compassion, you may be able to ease your parents' pain, but you cannot usually remove it. Some things you cannot change.

To be truly helpful to your parents, you must be able to see their problems clearly. The wisdom in the prayer depends in part on your capacity to balance thoughtfully and honestly not only the facts, but also the feelings of your parents as they grow frail and of yourself as you try to help them.

Is There a Problem?

Susie was telling the members of the support group about one of her ongoing dilemmas.

I struggle with how much to get involved in my mother's life. I know my sisters and even my husband think I worry too much. It started when my father got sick. Suddenly, my parents seemed old. I began to see problems everywhere and couldn't rest until I'd fixed them, or tried to.

Dad never really recovered from his prostate surgery — he had cancer — and just didn't have the energy to do much of anything. So Mum didn't do much either. She didn't complain, but I really thought she should be seeing friends and not stick at home just because he was. Staying indoors with a sick man is enough to make anyone depressed. And then there was the whole business of Dad's medical care. I got so frustrated. They never seemed to know what was going on. And of course they didn't want to bother their doctor by asking questions. I wrote down what I thought they should ask — what about a new drug I'd read about? should he have another CAT scan? — but they never did ask. Then, I'd bring in supplies from the health store — vitamins, and so on. I knew they'd never follow my advice but I couldn't stop myself.

It is worth standing back for a moment to take a clear view of what your parents face. What exactly are they dealing with? Sometimes there is no problem at all. You may be the one defining it as such.

There was no doubt that Susie's parents were having a difficult time, but they had no interest in handling things differently. They were satisfied with their doctor's care and, given the circumstances, her mother chose to stay home. Even big changes in your parents' lives do not signal problems in need of a solution. Susie's advice was unnecessary and possibly even irritating. There are times when it is better not to intervene.

More often than not, your parents will have some sadness about what is happening to them. A regret, however, is not the same as a serious problem. Certainly they would like to do what they have always been able to do, but most of the time, they are more reconciled to making adjustments than their children who want them to be forever vigorous. Your father may have given up some chores that have become difficult for him; it does not mean he has given up on life. Vacuuming may be a heavy task for your mother, but for her, the struggle may be a small price for the pride she has in continuing to care for her own home. Watching, as you have to do, may be the harder job.

Because most of us see the world from our own perspective we instinctively try to persuade others to do what we would do, or think we would, in their situation. We want what we think is best for them. The "we think" is a cue that we might think again. Your advice to your parents may range from the small ("You should get a microwave") to the monumental ("It's time to sell your house"). The suggestions may be good, appropriate, and made with the best of intentions, but that does not ensure that they fit your parents' situation or wishes.

Here is another example. The daughter of a seventy-three-year-old woman telephoned me to relate that her mother had undergone a personality change. She had become irritable, critical, and intolerant. The daughter described her mother as a person who always saw her glass as half empty, but she had never been negative to this degree. When did this start? Soon after her mother came to live with her daughter and her family. Since she moved in, life at home had become unpleasant for all. Three months earlier, the daughter continued, her mother had been widowed. She began to telephone frequently, complaining bitterly of her loneliness. Within six weeks, the daughter had packed up her mother's belongings and moved her into the spare room in her own house. At the time it seemed the caring thing to do.

When I met with the mother, it was clear that she felt more like the victim than the recipient of help. As she saw it, she had been whisked away from her home on a busy main street where she could sit in the window and watch the world's activity to a house where she was alone all day, where the windows looked out on the woods of rural New England, and where nothing moved. Not only was she more isolated, but she also resented the fact that the family was so busy that no one seemed to have time for her.

This family, with the best of intentions, had misidentified the problem. Caring is clearly a prerequisite to helping. But caring in itself is not sufficient. You must first really understand what the problem is. If you fail to grasp the issues involved, you may actually make a situation worse: the helping hand strikes again, as a friend of mine put it. The problem was not the mother's living situation so much as the loss of her husband and her own need to make adjustments to life alone.

When trying to assess whether or not your parents have a problem requiring your help, take as much time as possible. If you can tolerate the discomfort long enough to ask a lot of questions and consider alternatives, your solutions are more likely to be ones that are truly the best for your parents.

Whose Problem?

As Susie continued, she was more able to identify the difference between her issues and her parents'.

Looking back, half the things I worried about were not problems for my parents. For instance, the fact that they never went out. While I was at work, I'd be preoccupied by this picture of my parents sitting at home, seeing nobody except each other, unhappy and discouraged. In fact, they adjusted to Dad's poor health pretty well. Obviously they did not like what was happening to them, but they didn't see themselves as badly off as I did. He wasn't in pain and for the most part, they seemed content to be together.

But it was a problem for me. I felt compelled to visit them every few weeks to see for myself how they were doing. I used to ask myself why I went so often. They really didn't need help, but I felt I cheered them up and gave them new things to think and talk about.

Mom's problems nearly drove me crazy, though. She complained incessantly about the neighbors. There were several elderly women who, over the years, had come to depend on Mom and Dad for a variety of things — from making telephone calls to shopping, or advice on their Social Security. While Mom was irked by these requests, she never let on to the people who made them. I could have made a tape of myself telling her how she could politely say "no." I was surprised how angry I got on her behalf.

I fantasized that neighbors would come to the house while I was there so that I could tell them in no uncertain terms that they must stop taking advantage of my parents' good nature. Meanwhile, Mom continued to answer the doorbell and honor each request that came with it.

When we truly care about others, it is difficult to separate our feelings from theirs. We expect them to feel as we do. When we find a situation burdensome or uncomfortable, we assume they do too. We may be wrong. The people we love may find their situation quite tolerable or at least less intolerable than we do on their behalf. As Susie listened to her mother talk about her neighbors, she gradually realized that her mother did not really want the relationship to change. She occasionally felt burdened, it was true, but more than that she felt good that people still depended on her and that she was still needed. While Susie's advice about saying "no" was well meant, it was not, in fact, needed.

There may be occasions when your parents make decisions that are comfortable for them but not for you. A ninety-year-old friend of mine lives alone in a large house, situated half a mile from her nearest neighbor. She is physically frail but mentally very alert. She knows her limitations and moves around her home slowly, always with a hand on a piece of furniture. One evening, however, she went to sit down, missed the chair, and slid gently to the floor. She could not get up. She was not discovered for twenty-four hours. When rescued, my friend was hungry and uncomfortable but unhurt and remarkably unruffled. Her neighbors and daughter were not as calm. The consensus was that it was time for her to think about moving to Boston to join her daughter. She is an outspoken, intelligent, and forceful woman who left no one in any doubt that she was going to remain where she was and, what was more, no one was going to move in with her. She would rather take the risk of falling and being undiscovered than lose her independence. To allay concerns, she did agree to phone a nearby friend each evening so that there was a check at least once in twenty-four hours. More than that she was not prepared to do. Clearly, we have more of a problem with her living alone than she does. She is well aware of the risks but, for her, the price of avoiding them is too high. And the rest of us have to respect that.

Like my neighbor, your parents will probably endure a great deal to remain in their own home. If they are frail you may be concerned about their ability to take care of themselves, eat proper meals, avoid falling. From their point of view, they see only that they need to be more careful, to eat snacks instead of cooking meals, to accept the risks and stay where they are as long as possible. Your concern is natural, but do not panic into planning a move. As long as they are reasonably safe, it is more important that they retain control over their lives.

Another aspect of your parents' lives that you may want to change is their relationship with each other. In all probability, there's nothing you can do and you should think very carefully before you even try.

As far as I could tell my parents had always got on well. Certainly if they had any difficulties, we kids never saw them. Not that I'd want their kind of marriage—you know what I mean: Dad drove, Mom cooked; she decided what to buy, he gave her the money— but it worked well for them. That is, until Dad began to fail. Then I noticed for the first time how dependent she was on him. I was repeatedly making suggestions that must have irritated her. "Why don't you go out with a friend sometimes?" "Ask Dad to tell you how to manage your finances." Even, "How about learning to drive?" She never seemed annoyed but nor did she do anything differently.

Relationships come in an infinite variety, but, like Susie, some of you may not like what you see as you watch your parents. They may be dependent on each other, inconsiderate, or even quarrelsome. They may never have shown much affection or patience, but now that they are old and spend most of their time together, their unhappiness is more evident. And you notice it more. Sometimes it is the changes of old age — ill health, forgetfulness — that stress a formerly happy relationship. People who lived together in relative harmony often become irritable or resentful under extraordinary demands. Worse is when one parent seems to be victimized by the other. Perhaps a father who has always been controlling is now autocratic when he has no one but your mother to order around. Or a mother who resents having spent her life looking after people may be negligent and even unkind when she has to care for your disabled father.

It is uncomfortable if one of your parents makes you a confidante and complains to you about the other; it also feels inappropriate. However hard you try, you can rarely avoid the appearance of siding with one parent. If you do sympathize with one, and you often do, you may tempted to intervene. Few of us are immune to the feelings that come with being valued, especially by our parents. Whether you lecture, plead, or advise, however, your attempts to improve their relationship usually backfire. You annoy one and find that the other wanted only an interested ear and an ally. Neither wanted to hear suggestions about counseling, being more assertive, communicative. At worst, both parents see your good intentions as interference.

If your parents are unwilling to take some step themselves toward changing their unsatisfactory relationship, you can do little about it. Listening to your parents may help them cope more easily with a trying situation but, beyond that, it is usually advisable to resist the impulse to step in. In extreme situations, you may need to point out that it is intolerable for you to be torn between the two of them and you will not participate in any conversation that puts you in the middle. You then have to be true to your word and refuse to be drawn in.

In the final recourse, you have to accept that your parents have lived together for a long while and continue to choose to do so. The relationship might seem awful from outside but it must hold more satisfaction and comfort for them than the prospect of change. Marriages often look worse to others than to the participants. This is particularly true where two generations view the relationship between husband and wife differently. Your parents grew up with certain expectations of how to relate to each other, who makes what decisions and who accedes, and over decades of living together they have accommodated to each other and developed a system that works for them. You cannot see the whole picture. You may see your mother submitting to your father's apparently autocratic decisions whereas she knows that she has considerable influence by making quiet suggestions but refraining from challenging him. While you may cringe as your father is nagged by your mother, he may know that her irritation passes quickly, especially if he does not answer back.

Some problems are difficult to evaluate and painful to deal with. It is particularly worrying if one of your parents is sick or frail and the other seems to be giving incompetent or unkind care. If your vulnerable parent is at risk and suffering from lack of supervision or treatment, then someone has to intervene. On the other hand, if what you observe is occasional snappiness and complaining, your parents may not be unduly uncomfortable. People who have lived together contentedly for many decades are usually understanding of short temper and moodiness in the other. Watching and listening to them, you may find the situation uncomfortable but they may be used to it and certainly prefer it to any alternative.

In most instances, when you identify problems, it is out of concern for your parents' welfare, but on occasion, there may be other feelings too. You may be surprised if you feel disapproving, even jealous or angry. The problem may be entirely yours. It is easy to admire your father who regains his zest for life after your mother has died, but how do you feel when he starts to date and consider marrying again? While you like to see your mother going out with friends and playing golf, what do you think about her lack of interest in spending much time with your children? There is a large part in most of us that wants our parents not to change, to be predictable, and to be available to us. We may be concerned about our parents' behavior not so much because it brings them unhappiness, but because we have a sense of losing something we value.

Is There a Solution?

Now that Mom lives near me I still worry. Perhaps even more. She is so lonely since Dad died. I think I should be doing more but don't know what. I thought she'd be over his death by now. I've introduced her to one or two of my older friends and offered to go with her to the Senior Center, but she only shows interest in being with us. I do hate her being unhappy.

Your mother is lonely after your father dies and may feel that way for the rest of her life; your father may never feel as valued after he retired as when he was employed; your parents may never be happy together. You cannot solve their problems. Instead of the satisfaction of doing something practical, the only real help you may be able to give is to listen and be supportive. It is not always an easy role but it is often the most valuable.

Love and care cannot be measured by actions. You may imagine that relatives or neighbors are critical of your failure to *do* more for your parents. And you may be right. It is not uncommon to hear people praise an adult son or daughter for "doing so much" or criticize another for "letting her mother live alone." Even parents sometimes boast how much their child *does* for them in terms that correlate visible care and attention with love. You too may feel less guilty if you take action. Caring is not synonymous with doing, however. Indeed, sometimes, the most caring thing is to do nothing. Your presence and interest — in short, yourself — is the most precious gift you offer.

When to Step In

Susie thought about when she first had to take charge of some important aspect of her parents' lives.

Our relationship changed when Dad became very sick. When he was dying, really.

Mom did a great job of caring for him, but on the business side of things she was hopeless. She hadn't a clue about their finances, insurance policies, anything like that. Poor Mom. The thought of dealing with that stuff threw her into a panic. And they hadn't even signed a power of attorney or living will. So I took over all that. It took a lot of sorting out because things had got pretty disorganized since Dad got sick. I spent a lot of time on the phone, and with their accountant and lawyer.

"When do I take over?" "When do I decide that I know what is best for my parent?" These are some of the most poignant questions that you ever have to answer. If and when that point arrives, you are forced to recognize that your relationship with your parents has irrevocably changed. The people you depended on for many years now rely on you. You will probably feel uncomfortable at the very least. It is not a responsibility that you want — for yourself or for them. "I don't want to be a parent to my parent" is a natural response.

If you and your parents are fortunate, it may never be necessary for you to take over. Your parents may turn to you for advice or assistance with specific problems but they will not need you to make decisions for them. But if you are reading this, you have probably already decided that your parents do have a problem and cannot fully help themselves. How do you decide when, and how, to step in?

Again, there are few clear landmarks. There are different degrees of need, ranging from the parent who asks for help appropriately, to the parent who needs help but will not accept it, to the mentally impaired parent who needs total care and is unable to recognize it.

Normally independent people frequently suffer a crisis of self-confidence as they try to deal with the infirmities and losses that accompany aging. They may not travel for fear of getting sick away from home. They may avoid social events because they are embarrassed when they forget names or fail to hear all of a conversation. Fear can be crippling. One of my clients described her struggle with making decisions, in this case about money. Her husband had always been in charge of their finances, but since his stroke, he was incapable of doing so. Intellectually, she thought she was probably up to the task, but emotionally she felt completely intimidated. She repeatedly asked her daughter to make the decisions. What she really wanted, however, was someone to share in the decisions rather than make them unilaterally. When both realized that, the daughter offered to spend a morning with her regularly. Knowing that she could depend on those few hours, my client felt less out of her depth and regained some of her self-confidence. She needed help and asked for it, and her daughter responded appropriately.

Many problems are less easy to solve, not because there are no solutions but because your parents will not accept them. Your parents may have reached a stage when simple support is not enough. They have become sufficiently impaired physically or mentally that they are unable to care for themselves as they have in the past. They may be unsteady on their feet, avoid cooking, or forget appointments. They recognize their decline but steadfastly refuse assistance. Persuasion, nagging, begging, lecturing, all prove to be useless. You may be able to make help acceptable if you alter your approach.

Try to understand what is behind your parents' refusal. Do they think that accepting help signifies the first step to a nursing home? Is help being offered in an aggressive way that leaves them feeling personally diminished? Do they prefer to manage alone despite the potential dangers to their health and safety? If you can understand their reaction, you will be able to be more sensitive to their needs and be more effective.

At some point, you and your parents will have to decide what level of risk is tolerable. You will all make slightly different judgments about whether your parents are acceptably safe driving a car, cooking, staying alone. While you can voice your opinions and may have much influence, the choice ultimately belongs to your parent unless they are too confused to make rational decisions. Your conversations with your parents will be a great deal calmer if they take place before a crisis occurs. My elderly friend, who could not get up after a fall, was able to explain that for her the risk of falling was an acceptable price to pay for living in her own home. She could hear her daughter's concerns, however, and so agreed to the plan of a daily telephone check.

If your parents are truly incapable of caring for themselves, at some point you will have to step in and make decisions that are often unwanted, upsetting, and painful for everyone. There are some undeniable danger signals. Your mother frequently burns pots on the stove and does not notice, or is found wandering outdoors at 2:00 a.m., dressed only in nightclothes. Your father continues to drive his car although he loses his way in familiar surroundings. What makes these situations particularly difficult is that the people in such trouble usually have no recognition that they have a problem — indeed, have no memory of being lost or no sense that they are confused. You are then obliged to take some action that will bring unhappiness. Your parents may not understand the reason for intervention and resent it. You are acting in their best interests but regarded as an ogre for doing so. This is one of the most difficult stages in caring for your parents.

Role Reversal

If your parents are no longer competent to make their own decisions or care for themselves, you have to take over many tasks similar to those your parents once did for you — deciding where to live, how to spend money, and, ultimately, helping with eating and toileting. Your roles have apparently reversed. You may describe yourself as parenting your parents. While there is some truth to it, it is a concept with unfortunate implications. In reality, our parents are never our children. They continue to think of themselves as capable, knowledgeable, and nurturing and are usually acutely sensitive to signs that they are not. The danger and consequences of patronizing older people are immense.

However impaired in old age, your parents have lived many decades as adults in control of their own lives. Even the most confused seem to sense that there is something amiss when they cannot look after themselves. They are embarrassed by signs of failure, such as incontinence, and often troubled by needing help with basic tasks, such as dressing. When they are treated by others, whether their children or staff in a nursing home, in manner, words, or tones normally reserved for young children, their dignity and self-esteem are seriously threatened.

Unpopular Decisions

When you provide practical care to your parents, they usually see you as helpful or at least as having good intentions. They are likely to regard you very differently if you have to impose restrictions on them because their safety demands it. Then you may be seen as unreasonable, misguided, or, at worst, tyrannical.

One issue raised time and time again by children concerned about their aging parents is that of driving. In this culture, driving a car not only means mobility but is synonymous with maturity and independence. To give up the car keys feels like giving up part of one's identity as an adult. Occasionally, people can recognize that they are no longer safe behind the wheel of a car or can be persuaded to let someone else do the driving. More often, they see no reason to stop, and you and your family agonize about how to get them off the road without devastating their feelings or precipitating an argument.

Driving is just one activity that is an emotionally laden symbol of competence and self-worth. There are many others — cooking, handling money, living alone — which some older people have to give up as they grow frail. How willingly they hand them over varies considerably from person to person. Some people resist every inch of the way, never becoming reconciled to their diminishing capabilities, whereas others accept that it is time to hand over some responsibilities. You can make a difference by the way you handle the situation. Patience and empathy are crucial. If you can be sensitive to the meaning of a particular activity, you convey an understanding that makes your parents better able to deal with the loss. Saving face is another balm we all use to make difficult situations more comfortable. Your parents are often open to suggestions that certain actions, or cessation of certain activities, will be a relief to you. They may find it tolerable to give up driving, or handling their finances if they think that it will ease your mind by doing so. The notion that the decision has more to do with pleasing their children than reflecting their diminished skills may be important for them.

Sometimes it is more comfortable for everyone if you can enlist an outside authority to suggest or even enforce restrictions. If your parents are in a potentially dangerous situation and will not listen to you, it is time to look for other resources and to consider whether some other person or agency could better help with specific problems. In the case of driving, for example, a word from the police or a physician has much more influence on a parent who is determined to use a car than the opinion of a child. A parent who is no longer safe living alone can be gently told by the landlord or a social worker. And exasperating though it may be to admit, one of your siblings may be better equipped than you to handle certain matters. If you feel awkward, look carefully around you for the person best able to take on a particular issue.

Professionals may be useful not only in enforcing unpopular decisions but also in taking on identified tasks. For your own sake, you need to use whatever help exists. Your parents may also find it easier to accept help from people in some official capacity than from their own family. If they cannot pay their own bills, for example, they may feel less disenfranchised if their bank or accountant takes over. They might also be more comfortable being bathed by a home health aide than by their children. Professional resources are usually limited, but when available they can take considerable strain off you and the relationship between you and your parents.

Caregiving at a Distance

The most difficult time for me was the two years when my father was sick. My parents lived four hours away, so when I visited, which I felt I had to do every two or three weeks, I was gone the whole weekend. My life was split between two homes — my parents' and my own. More and more, it was their world that was taking over. Even when I wasn't with them physically, I was thinking about them, worrying how they were managing. It was hard on my husband and kids too; I just wasn't there for them.

One of the problems for me was that Mom wouldn't ask for help. Things could be pretty bad and I wouldn't know until I got there. She always insisted she was okay, but the truth was that she was becoming exhausted with all the extra work she had to do as Dad got sicker. But no way was she going to have a stranger come into her house to help her. I produced every argument I could think of. I don't know what made the difference, but she finally agreed to at least meet someone from the health service. I rushed to the phone before she changed her mind.

Geographic mobility is a characteristic of our time. In no generation have so many adult children and their parents lived so far from each other.

This physical distance has implications even when our parents are healthy. Our children miss a close relationship with their grandparents. Our parents are unable to watch their grandchildren growing up. Living too far away for brief visits, we may have to use vacation time to see them, which sometimes — logistically and emotionally — produces more stress than pleasure all around.

If you and your parents live at some distance, the telephone is probably your main link. Though inadequate to deal with complex emotional issues, it is an expedient way to communicate and to convey your interest and concern. And your parents may need support and contact more than your physical presence. This is especially true if they live alone or are caring for a sick partner. What they need most to know is that you are interested enough to make regular contact, to listen, and to try to understand. The desire to be known and appreciated is universal. The telephone can be a wonderfully effective instrument for conveying loving attention, bridging short or vast distances. Do not ever underestimate the value of making that effort. It may seem so simple as to be superficial — but it can be extremely important to your parents.

As your parents' frailty grows more pronounced, geographic distance becomes not only an inconvenience but a problem. Then you dread the call that may announce a crisis. The telephone is an unsatisfactory means of communication when you have to assess an emergency. Yet this is what you have to do. Planned visits become a luxury of the past. You have to rely on the phone to determine if your presence is really required or if you can settle things from home. It is useful to know your parents' friends, neighbors, and doctor. With your parents' permission, you might get to know a few key people, so that you have someone to call to help you evaluate the situation. Make sure they also have your name and number.

Like all families, you and your parents have had many years to develop and practice ways of behaving toward each other. By the time your parents are old, these patterns have become second nature and are difficult to change. It is common, for example, for parents to protect their children from unpleasant realities ("They have enough problems to deal with") or to be unwilling to ask for help ("There's nothing they can do anyway"). If your parents hide their difficulties, you know only one thing for certain: that you do not know the whole story. If you too are not entirely straightforward, your parents are also in the dark about what you can do, given your other commitments. You both fill in the gaps by guessing, which rarely produces a mutually satisfactory outcome. The game of second-guessing leads to endless confusion, and nowhere is it more confusing than for family members who must communicate long-distance. It is only when each of you can rely on the other to be open and honest that you stand a chance of assessing a situation correctly. Without relevant information, neither of you can hope to act appropriately or effectively.

One of my clients found that his mother's phone calls increased both in frequency and urgency as his father's condition declined progressively with Alzheimer's disease. At first, the son responded to his mother's obvious distress by making a five-hour drive in an attempt to sort out the problem. After several such visits, he realized that he could not maintain such a schedule. Nor did it provide what his mother needed. She could, in fact, handle most of the practical problems. Her real struggle was living with the loss of her companion and partner of fifty years. The son and his mother were able to talk about their respective dilemmas. Each had some appreciation of the other's situation, and they were able to settle on a workable solution — at least for the time being. They arranged to talk on the telephone when both had time for an unhurried conversation. By talking regularly, the son was able to keep abreast of daily developments and to more accurately gauge the seriousness of his mother's need. For her part, she felt much better able to cope knowing that her son was an involved and willing listener.

Unless you are an only child, your brothers and sisters are part of the picture. Ideally, you all work together to decide what help your parents need and what each of you can contribute. Again, difficulties are compounded when you live at a considerable distance from each other. You have to work at keeping each other informed, cooperating with each other, asking for and offering help. One or more of your siblings may be unwilling or unable to do their share, but if you do not tell them when problems exist there is certainly less chance that they will be available.

How Much Can I Do?

Mom's move has not been as successful as I thought it would be. Some things have worked out well. Mom and the kids love each other, which is a real plus. But she's made no life for herself.

What should I do? Visit more often? I'm there every day as it is. Invite her to live with us? But that would mean we'd have to build an addition, and I'm not sure it's a good idea anyway. What can I expect — of her, of me? To tell you the truth, I sometimes wonder when I'll have time for me.

In addition to deciding what your parents need, you have to decide what you personally can do. The answer is different for each of you. You have to look at the different aspects of your lives, your responsibilities, abilities, physical and emotional energy, and then work out a balance that comes closest to meeting the needs of all, including yourself.

You do not have to do everything. In most communities there is some help available especially for concrete tasks such as housework, bathing, delivered meals. Services vary and frequently require persistence and skill to identify, but the effort is usually worthwhile. Your parents may balk at first, and unless you enlist their cooperation, they may cancel your careful arrangements as soon as your back is turned. Take time to understand their point of view. They may be unwilling to pay for a service they do not think they need or to accept aid from strangers. You can encourage them to realize that you need help too. If you can remain clear and firm, your parents' resistance will probably slowly thaw as what seemed an impersonal service becomes a friendly and familiar person.

For many of you, your parents' needs are emotional rather than practical. Susie, for example, felt badly that her mother was unhappy. She wished that it was practical help that she needed. Concrete tasks have a beginning and an end. Her mother's loneliness did not have a solution that Susie could see. Whatever the demands, you have to decide what you are able to do and let go of expectations that are beyond your resources.

Whatever action you take, the result is usually a compromise. Deciding if, when, and how to help are questions that continue throughout your parents' old age. Your answers will change as new circumstances arise. Few solutions are perfect. You go as far as possible toward meeting the needs of all for the present but invariably you will soon face a new dilemma. It may be more difficult to deal with, it may be easier, but it will be different. This is an ongoing process, moving from one compromise to another, answering each problem as best you can.

Points to Consider

1. Understand your parents' problems before you think about doing anything to solve them.

2. Understanding, interest, and compassion may be more important than action.

3. Ask yourself whether your parents' struggles, losses, and pains are more difficult for you than for them.

4. Most older people will do much to retain some control over their lives. To remain independent, they may be prepared to make many compromises in the way they live. In evaluating their decisions, try to see the situation from their point of view and allow for as much autonomy as the situation permits.

5. Talk to your parents while they are still healthy about what help they would find acceptable if they become frail.

6. If your parents become incompetent and unable to care for themselves safely, you may have to take on the responsibility or ensure that someone else does so.

7. Some professionals or agencies may help assess your parents' situation and be more effective in imposing necessary restrictions on such activities as driving and living alone.

8. Become familiar with agencies that provide services to the elderly.

9. Try to be honest with parents, siblings, and yourself — honest about what you think needs to be done, what you can do, and what help you need. Encourage other family members to talk openly too, so that everyone sees the situation and its potential solutions as clearly as possible.

10. Older people, however impaired, deserve to be treated with respect and dignity.

11. There are few ideal solutions. Most are compromises.

· Chapter 4 ·

What Action to Take

PLANNING IS FUN when you think about a vacation or a party, but as you look ahead to your parents' old age, you are more likely to feel apprehension or even dread. How much will your parents need you? How will you cope? Will you have to help them move house, admit them to a nursing home, handle their affairs? There is no pleasure in anticipating any of these things.

My mother's been living with us for two years, since she had a stroke. It's gone reasonably well up to now. Or at least I thought it had. I knew I was tired — I always am — but who isn't? A friend visited last month, though, and told me I looked and acted extremely stressed. I realized that was true, but I hadn't thought it was visible to anyone else. It sort of alarmed me.

What worried Martha was the level of her stress now and how she would handle problems in the future. Both concerns had brought her to the group.

I don't want to look ahead because I see more and tougher problems. Mom is at high risk for another stroke. Even without that, she's less able to care for herself than when she first came to live with us. If she continues to go downhill, I don't know what we'll do. Will I have to give up my job? I don't see how we could employ help. Should I think about a nursing home? How much more can I ask of my husband and sons?

It is tempting not to plan for an unknown future. After all, what you fear may never happen and meanwhile you become unnecessarily depressed and anxious.

Despite such resolves, we often worry anyway. Unbidden, our ruminations about our parents and their care interrupt our sleep in the predawn hours. Gradually, we, or other people, notice that signs of stress have taken root.

Even without a crystal ball, without knowing what to anticipate, planning does have some advantages. Unlike worrying, it does make us better prepared for what might come. Life has many unknowns, but change itself is a certainty. We can reasonably predict that health, mobility, and the ability to be independent will decline in old age. Looking ahead, thinking about specific contingencies, talking about future alternatives helps us to be ready in case we need to be.

One caution: while it is prudent to think about possible difficulties, do not act as if they have already materialized. Rather, think in terms of beginning with the smallest step necessary to deal with any problem that arises. If your parents' garden becomes too much of a chore, for example, they can think first of employing help before considering a major move. Encourage them to consider small adjustments rather than large and disruptive revisions.

Try to employ the same economy of action in your own planning. If your parents become frail and needy, you will almost certainly be involved in some way. You need to know what you can and cannot do and how you can take care of yourself as well as them.

Stress for the Caregiver

After my friend's visit, I took a good look at myself. And I didn't like what I saw. I already knew that I wasn't sleeping well. Then one night Mom fell in the bathroom. Since then, I wake at the first sound from her room, and I don't get back to sleep for hours. It seems that I never relax. If I'm not working, I'm thinking about what I need to do next. And I scarcely ever go out with my husband or the boys. I'm too tired or I think I should stay home with Mom since she rarely leaves home.

Even my personality seems to have changed. My sense of humor has disappeared. I don't know when I last really laughed. I'm thankful for my job. Even there though, when I do have time to talk, the conversation invariably comes around to my situation at home and all that I have to do. I'm becoming a bore!

I feel like I should be coping much better than I am. Sure, Mom needs help and that means extra work for me, but is that so much to deal with? She rarely complains or asks for help unless she really needs it. Our relationship is really good, and I know enough not to take that for granted. But I do feel guilty that I sometimes long to come home to an empty house where no one needs anything, not even conversation.

There have been innumerable studies of the burden of caring for elderly people and the effect upon those who give the care. The general conclusion is unanimous: caring for frail older relatives is stressful. Most caregivers report one or more of an array of symptoms. Fatigue, depression, nervousness, headaches, muscle tension, irritability are just the most common signs of emotional strain. Like Martha, you may be preoccupied by your parents, talking about them in every conversation. If you notice that you have increased your use of alcohol, tranquilizers, or sleeping pills, that your sleep or eating habits have changed, you should ask for help.

Of all groups caring for the elderly, daughters report the most stress — more than spouses and much more than sons. Generally speaking, women are cued into their parents' overall needs and take responsibility for whatever needs to be done, whether it is cleaning, transporting, personal care, talking, or listening. For you in particular, however, whether you are a son or daughter, your sense of stress increases along with the amount of help you provide. Even good relationships become strained as your parents need more attention and you have less time to give it. This is especially true if your parents have a dementing illness which makes them confused, forgetful, and sometimes uncooperative.

You cannot take on extensive responsibility for your frail parents without altering your own lives. You may have to give up vacations, leisure, time alone or with friends. The feeling of being trapped, of your time not being your own, is generally more of a strain than the *amount* of work you do. Jobs that can be scheduled and completed usually bring some sense of accomplishment. But to be constantly on call, never knowing when the next request or problem will arise, is stressful indeed.

There is plenty of evidence that emotional stress affects not just our minds, but our bodies too. When we see something to be anxious about, our brains send messages to our bodies. Adrenaline outputs increase, hearts beat faster, and energy floods in to the large muscles. This response — often referred to as the primitive "fight or flight response" — worked well when a hairy mammoth came round the corner of the prehistoric landscape but is less effective in dealing with the pressures of modern life. Physical fight or flight are often not viable options for dealing with our current problems. And with no active outlet available, anxiety turns inward. Over time, we pay the price with emotional stress and, ultimately, with physical illness. It has been known for a long time that those who experience major disruptions in their lives, such as death of a spouse, divorce, or sudden unemployment, have a greater risk of becoming ill in the year following the change. Less traumatic, but chronic, anxieties carry similar hazards.

Stress is not reserved for major events. A large number of minor hassles can erode our calm and flexibility. If you are responsible for your parent, you cannot predict or control the demands, challenges, and expectations on you. Each request may be minor in itself but the accumulation can be considerable. "Does that awful Medicare form have to be filled in today?" "Does his cat really need to go to the veterinarian?" "What are the kids doing while I am helping her into the car?" "How can I tell them we won't be coming for Thanksgiving?" Your blood pressure can rise in mere anticipation.

One problem with minor hassles is that you may think you should not be bothered by them. You do not feel good about complaining, even to yourself. Can you feel justified in being angry that your mother walks slowly, that your father presses you to pay every bill for him as soon as it arrives, or that traffic was heavy or your children's choice of music was jarring, all in one afternoon? Here is where stress has a field day.

We all deal with stress in different ways. Indeed we even define it differently. What is an anxiety for me may be a challenge for you. What makes you feel overwhelmed someone else may take in stride. It is a valid argument that all of us benefit from some degree of stress. Just as exercising muscles makes them more powerful, so does emotional challenge make us stronger and more resilient. For stress to stand a chance of being beneficial, however, we need to have some sense of being able to handle it. We can see ourselves reflected in those unpleasant experiments in which researchers give electric shocks to laboratory animals: the animals that are given random shocks become nervous and neurotic, while those who can learn to avoid the shock by pressing a lever remain emotionally stable. If we try to think about our complex lives, we know that we deal with the tasks we *choose* to undertake so much more easily than unsolicited or unplanned demands to which we feel we cannot say "no."

Coping with Stress

Your stress is real, and failing to attend to it rarely makes it better. It is not your imagination, nor a sign of moral degeneration. Feeling badly about feeling bad becomes a vicious circle. Telling yourself that you should be strong enough to cope, or that nothing can be done to ease your situation, closes off possible help. With some thought, there is usually something you can do, if not to eliminate the stress, at least to reduce it.

It is essential that you give some thought to your own mental and physical health. This is not selfishness. If you are exhausted, irritable, or agitated, you are not doing *anyone* much good. Others' welfare, including your parents', depends on your staying in good shape, emotionally and physically. Many frail people are admitted to nursing homes primarily because the family members who were looking after them have become sick and exhausted. Looking after yourself becomes your first responsibility.

One key to your mental health is a sense of control. As I mentioned earlier, most of us feel better if we feel we have some choice about what we do. If you are feeling stressed, you might take a long, calm look at what you are doing to ascertain whether you can simplify or reduce your commitments. Small adjustments in your routine can make a world of difference. The trick is to identify the elements of your routine that can be changed without creating new problems to deal with. Can you cut down on the frequency of some tasks? Can someone cover for you once in a while? Can you set aside time for your own interests and pleasures?

Many of you probably ask the impossible of yourself. The reality is that there are limits to what you can do for your elderly parents. No one can replace their lost loves, lifetime companions, or many of the activities that gave meaning and pleasure to their lives. You can drive yourselves to the point of exhaustion by trying to ensure that your parent is never sad or lonely. In dealing with an emergency you may give a great deal of time and effort, but you cannot keep that up over the long haul. You have to pace yourselves. The quality of your care is only as great as your capacity to give. And your capacity to give is bounded by your own reserves.

You may find it easier to be relaxed and patient if you think about what is really important in your contact with your parents. What aspect of your interaction matters most? Any activity has several meanings. If you choose to see a shopping expedition as an outing with your mother rather than as a chore to get through as quickly as possible, your expectations will be different and your frustration reduced. Working alongside your father in the garden may be less efficient than working alone, but the companionship may be more important than the actual job you do.

Whenever people feel overwhelmed, the first thing they give up is looking after themselves. You no longer seem to have time for lunch with a friend, a quiet interlude with a good book. It is this kind of thing that replenishes you, however, even more so in times of stress. Every one of you has different ways of being good to yourself, and though it is difficult to fit them into a busy schedule, it is vital to do so. Build time for yourself into your life. The anticipation of a walk with a friend, a lazy bath, time alone in the garden — each can give lasting benefit.

The most valuable coping skill of all is a sense of humor. Anger and frustration are almost always dissipated by laughter. Remember that your parents are as frustrated by their incapacities and frailties as you are — probably more so — but sharing the humorous side can take out the sting. If you can see the ridiculous side of having to help your mother bathe or your father dress, you all relax.

Support groups can be wonderful places to meet others who have similar experiences and frustrations. The process of hearing and being heard is a powerful one. Most people leave the sessions with a lighter sense of burden and a clearer perspective on their situation. You may be reticent about talking about your difficulties to your families and friends, concerned that you complain too much or that they cannot understand. Your reluctance can be set aside in a support group because everyone is in a similar situation, is interested, and shares many of the same feelings. The hesitant admission of being snappy on occasion is typically greeted by much head-nodding around the circle. There is a healing quality of empathy and recognition that can restores one's sense of humor and proportion. It is definitely worth a try if you can find an appropriate group.

Getting the Help You Need

Accepting help is difficult for many of us. We think that we should be able to manage alone, that to need help is some sign of failure. Consequently, we are reluctant to ask, saying that we do not want to burden others, that we can cope, that we are afraid of being a nuisance. Yet, accepting help and asking for it are essential skills if you are not to become burned out. It may make it easier for you to remember that just as you are usually happy to *give* help, so will be the people who care about you. By refusing to accept help, you are not only making life more burdensome for yourself, but you also fail to give others a valuable opportunity to stand with or by you.

It may irritate you to think that you have to do the asking. You may think, with some justification, that others, especially members of your family, should see that you need help and take the initiative. Unfortunately, people are often not that observant, or they may be reticent about offering, fearing to be intrusive. If you are one who is commonly seen as being in control, others may hesitate to approach you, unsure of how you will react.

When your friends and neighbors offer to help, they probably talk in general terms — "Let me know if there is anything I can do." There are some wonderful people who may see exactly what you need, but they are rare. Most want to help, but they do not know exactly what would help you most. You have to take the next step. When responding to such general offers, it is a good idea to be specific, citing particular examples of acts that you would appreciate. "Are you ever free to take Mum to the hairdresser?" Remember that small acts can make a big difference to you.

Respite

If you are much involved in the care of your parents, you need some respite from your responsibilities or you will become depleted. You need to know that you will have some time for yourself, whether it is a few hours, a few days, or even a number of weeks. If you cannot pull in a member of the family to take over care for a while, you may have to employ help. One of the deterrents to hiring help is that it does take time and effort to find suitable people, to interview them and introduce them to your parents. It may seem too much trouble. Once found, however, such help can be a godsend.

There are some agencies that provide respite. Unfortunately, in this country they are few and far between and are often expensive. Where they do exist, they are an important resource. Elderly day care programs also offer care and activities during the day, making it possible for caregivers to maintain their jobs and providing supervision and a social life for frail elderly people. Some Veterans' Administration hospitals provide overnight care to veterans, as do some nursing homes, but they are usually costly.

As you contemplate hiring help, you may discount it on the grounds that your parents will not accept it. And indeed, when they are comfortable with their surroundings and the person who cares for them, they are likely to resist any change. Why would they want to go to a strange place or spend time with an unfamiliar person? It is unrealistic to expect them to welcome such a plan, but if you are clear in your own mind that you need a break if you are to continue to provide quality care, your parents will probably respond to your clarity. They may be far from delighted that you are leaving, but they will accept it. If they are not confused, they may be able to appreciate that you cannot always be available. Sometimes they even feel good that they are helping *you* by allowing you some time for yourself. Parents tend to remain parents all their lives, and your parents are sometimes more understanding than you anticipate.

If your parents are confused, they will find a new routine less disturbing if you introduce it slowly. Visits from new helpers or to new places may go more smoothly if you stay around for a while until the strangeness wears off. Your choice of words can be important. Words such as "sitter" or "day care" are likely to have negative connotations, especially to people who do not understand why they cannot stay alone. Introduction of a new caregiver as someone who "would like to visit with you" or "is helping me with the housework" is more likely to be acceptable. With creativity and luck, you may be able to come up with substitute caregivers to whom your reluctant parent is likely to respond less negatively. Most often, you will have to be clear, consistent and gently firm until your parents become reconciled to the change.

Moving In

My husband and I didn't need much discussion before suggesting that Mom move in with us. We'd always known in the back of our minds that if she couldn't live alone then she'd live with us. I did check with my brothers and they accepted the plan with no question. After all, I'm the daughter. And Mom certainly didn't need a nursing home.

Before she arrived, most of our talk was about practical details. Which room would be hers? How would we arrange the other room to make space for both boys? Could we ask Mom to contribute financially?

In fact, the arrangement worked out well for quite a while. It's only lately that it's got hard. Even so, knowing what I now know, I'd make the same decision again. Having another person in the house, though, is more difficult than I'd anticipated, especially when they are old and frail. It is very different from having Mom for a vacation. The boys soon noticed that difference too. They were used to her being active and joining in almost everything we did, but now she finds it difficult to walk and tires easily. And with her weak arm she cannot dress herself completely, let alone help me out. Most of the extra work falls on me, of course. I hate to ask the rest of the family for help — after all, she's my mother — but they do have more chores these days than they used to.

Other changes weren't so obvious, though, and in many ways they're more difficult to deal with. This is now Mom's home, and she's part of our family. We can't say "Vacation's almost over. We'll soon be back to normal." We all have to put up with any inconvenience or irritation. And that's true for Mom too. However fond she is of us, living with us is not her first choice. You know she'd rather be in her place and be independent. It's a huge adjustment for us all. And we're lucky. We all like each other. I wonder how families manage who don't get on well.

To decide to have your parent moving in with you is an enormous decision, big enough to deserve serious attention on the part of everyone concerned. In an ideal world, you, your family, your siblings, and your parents are able to discuss the situation as each sees it. There is time, opportunity, honesty, and ability to consider the pros and cons of various alternatives. Of course, the ideal rarely exists. You may have to respond to a crisis, your siblings are estranged from each other, your parents are unable to understand what is happening to them. With some thought and talk, however, it is possible to increase the chance of making a decision that will work out well.

Occasionally, older people live with one of their children for no other reason except that both want it. A mother and a single child may decide to live together for companionship, economy, and convenience. A parent may move into a "granny flat" attached to the home of one child; she is healthy, quite independent and gives as much help as she receives.

In all probability, however, the suggestion that you and your parents live together emerges from their need. They cannot live alone. It is not a plan that either of you would choose unless forced to do so.

The vital question to ask first is "Does my parent need to move at all?" Many parents move, or are moved, and come to regret the decision, realizing too late that it was not really necessary. A mother who is feeling frightened and lonely after her husband has died does not necessarily need to leave her home. A father who has never learned to cook for himself does not have to live with someone else for that reason. There are ways of solving many problems that are less of an upheaval than you all sharing a house.

Under what circumstances do you take the next step of seriously considering living together? Carefully and realistically assess your parents' needs. Do they need more than social agencies, friends, and family can provide? Do you find that they are not safe and not able to care for themselves or their home, even with help? Do they require some help and supervision in order to be safe and comfortable?

What about your needs? These are as important as those of your parents. We are, after all, talking about people living together. For that to work for any one person it has to work reasonably well for everyone. If one person is unhappy or resentful of the arrangement, it will be difficult and stressful for all. Do you have the energy, time, and commitment to invite your parent in? What about the house? Is there room for another person? Can it accommodate someone who may have difficulty getting around? Problem areas tend to be stairs and bathrooms. What about privacy? Is there enough for everyone?

More important, how does everyone get on with each other? If your family and your parents find each other irritating or difficult whenever you spend more than a few days together, it is highly improbable that you will easily tolerate sharing the same living space. And you might be sharing it for a long while. Offering your parent a home out of a sense of obligation may relieve guilty feelings for a brief time, but an obligatory arrangement is rarely a comfortable one. Feelings not only enrich but also complicate every human interaction, and nowhere more so than in families. Being honest with yourself and each other before you act saves a great deal of heartache later.

You may plan to protect your family from the extra work and inconvenience of having your parent live with you, but, however hard you try, your family will be deeply affected. How does each member feel about the proposed plan? What do your children think? How their lives will be changed by the arrival of your parent will depend on many factors — their age, their relationship with their grandparent, and above all your ability to continue to give them the quantity and quality of attention they require. And what about your partners? Nothing is more important than their attitude. Your relationship suffers if you are not able to support and understand each other. Understanding is needed in both directions.

When someone is added to your family, especially when that person is related to you or your partner, your interactions with each other become more complicated. When your parent is in your home, you may feel in the middle whenever there is any conflict. Like Martha, you are caught between loyalty to your parent and your family. Acutely aware of the sensitivities of both sides you feel in a no-win position. If you are living with your partner's parents, you are probably less torn emotionally but may resent the time, attention, and space that they take. With another adult in the house, regardless of whose parent it is, couples have less time, privacy, and energy for fun, love-making, or conversation.

You are not the only ones having to make an adjustment. Moving in with their adult children is not easy for parents. Most older people no more choose to live with their children than children choose to have parents live with them. Given their preference, most older people would opt for living separate from, but near, their families. Moving in together is usually a solution to a problem, not a free choice. The move is hard for everyone.

It is difficult for old people to give up their own homes. Not only do they leave a familiar place with many memories, but they know they will never live independently again. While probably thankful that you care enough to make a home for them, your parents have many regrets that it is necessary. Part of them may feel burdened by their indebtedness to you, or they may resent having to be a permanent guest in someone else's home. Their new surroundings are likely to be much busier and more confusing than their own home in recent years. And you and your family are different when seen every day in all your moods and preoccupations. They may find themselves witnessing family quarrels that they would prefer not to know about. You may be less easy to live with than they thought — or than you think you are, for that matter. The challenge to adjust is considerable for everyone.

Parents who are confused have a special difficulty because they do not understand what is going on. For them it is a mystery why they are no longer living in their own house. They were not aware of having any problems. And your home may remain forever strange to them. For you, too, dementia poses a special challenge. Your parents' ability to adapt and comprehend is dramatically reduced. Every time they are uncomfortable, they may insist on returning home or resent that they were "taken away." Unable to understand or remember what is happening, they have no tools to help them adjust. They are unlikely to be capable of altering their behavior to fit in with other people, not because they are thoughtless by nature, but because they have lost the ability to put themselves in others' shoes. People with a dementia have diminished capacities for empathy and consideration of others. It is the healthy members of the family who have to take more of the responsibility for adapting and planning for things to go smoothly.

Even if you and your parents have every advantage on your side, there will be some difficult times. There are inevitable tensions. When you lived with them as a child, it was your parents who made the rules. As you reached adulthood and created your own homes and families, your parents probably became the visitors. Guests and hosts have to make adjustments, but only for the duration of the visit. Parents and children who live together, however, do not have that luxury. Because the arrangement is more or less permanent, difficulties have to be dealt with.

The best time to face potential problems is before your parent moves in. Not all conflicts can be predicted, but some can. What expectations do you and your parents have of each other? How much help does each of you need and expect? Is your parent going to contribute financially, and if so, how much? How much togetherness or time alone? Does your parent need help or company during the day, and if so, who will provide it? Some of these questions can be partially answered or at least aired before your parent moves in. You will probably want to consider them again after you have lived together for a while. To assume that parents and children can live together without tension fits in with the image of the ideal family, which we perhaps all carry somewhere inside us. It is certainly reinforced in the popular media, but it is a dangerous assumption. It is far better to recognize that there will be difficulties and adjustments for everyone.

Nursing Home

Mom had a second stroke and this one was worse. She couldn't walk. I kept hoping she'd improve — and her speech did — but her right arm and leg were useless. She needed help with everything. Getting in and out of bed, using the toilet, bathing were all beyond her without someone to lift her.

While she was still in the hospital, I got a call from the discharge nurse. Discharge! I couldn't believe they were even thinking about it. Well, they weren't. They thought Mom should go to a nursing home where she could get the care and therapy she needed. I felt really terrible. This is what I'd hoped to avoid. How could I tell her that she couldn't come home? What would she think? Looking back, I realize I clung to the word "therapy." Perhaps she'd regain enough strength to return home after a few weeks of treatment. Of course, I was mistaken, but it gave us both something to hold on to.

Nursing homes have a negative image in our culture — a dumping ground for old people whose families do not care. Like Martha, you may think of them as the place of last resort, where people are obliged to go when there is no one to look after them. Your parents may have mentioned their dread of ending up in "a home" and even asked you to promise that this will never happen to them. It is a promise that you may not be able to keep. Nursing homes exist for a purpose. They are there, not because families are unwilling to care for their frail members, but because they are not always capable of doing so. Yet the negative perception continues. Caught up in such feelings, you may delay using a service that both you and your parents need. Or if once that decision is made, you may be flooded with a sense of failure and guilt.

The reality of nursing homes may be different from your image. Certainly there are bad nursing homes where the staff appear uncaring and overworked, and the residents listless. But most nursing homes provide clean, cheerful surroundings, good physical care, and kind attention.

Unfortunately, nursing homes cannot avoid looking somewhat clinical because they do have to care for many people with disabilities and medical problems. You may be depressed by the sight of wheelchairs, walkers, and oxygen tanks, but many of the residents need them. Good nursing homes do much more than meet the residents' physical needs. They usually offer an active social program, outings for those who are well enough, and, above all, staff who show interest and love for the people in their care. In these specially designed surroundings, your frail elderly parents may possibly regain some of the independence and strength that they appeared to have lost. For people with a severe dementia, for instance, their homes may have become a frustrating and even dangerous places. Nursing homes with their predictable routines, specially planned activities, and environments that are designed to be safe and more simple often help people feel less confused and more relaxed. Your parents have to spend less energy struggling with situations they do not understand.

Nursing homes are part of the continuum of care. If the needs of the elderly are seen along a line that begins while they are living independently, extends through help at home, special housing with some supervision, and living with an adult child, it ends at a nursing home. Many old people do not need all of the services along this line, but some do. Nursing homes are set up to offer the comprehensive and skilled care that some people need but is rarely possible for family members to provide at home.

By the time you admit your parents to a nursing home, you have usually spent years helping them cope at home. Far from abdicating your responsibilities, you have done all, and sometimes more than, you were able. You have reached a point when you can no longer do it alone. Your parents must have resources designed to meet their needs and caregivers who are available around the clock.

You will not be able to predict when you will no longer be able to manage. That point comes at a different time and place for everyone. Coping is an individual characteristic, with so many variables that comparisons to others' situations are pointless. No one can truly appreciate another's situation. It is for each of you to decide what you can do, given your particular circumstances. And it is probably safe to say you will know it if and when the time comes for a nursing home.

You and your parents' situations will change. If you decide you can continue to manage without a nursing home, you need to evaluate your position periodically. Ask yourself how you are doing, how your family is faring, and whether your parents are still as comfortable as possible.

However pressing your circumstances, you will be unusual if you do not feel some guilt and distress if the time comes for you to place your parent in a nursing home. "She cared for me. Can't I do as much for her?" "If I were a better (stronger, more loving, responsible) person, I would provide the care myself." "Will he be cared for properly?" Each question is legitimate. In theory, you can always try more or postpone a decision a little longer. And in some ways, the care in a nursing home is not as good as it can be at home. It is not as personal, not delivered in comfortably familiar surroundings. Instead, it provides safety, essential medical equipment and care, round-the-clock supervision, and a trained staff. There comes a point when these may be more important to your parents' well-being than their own or your home. And it may be more important for you too. It is not easy to face that your parents need more than you can supply. Your love is not sufficient to make them comfortable. Even more difficult to accept is the knowledge that part of you no longer *wants* to look after them. Inside, there is a pocket of relief that someone else is taking on the main responsibility. *This is perfectly normal, perfectly okay.*

Your guilt will probably be short-lived, but you may feel a lingering sadness. Nursing home care marks a new stage. For your parents, their world has become a smaller place, restricted by ill health, mental confusion, or lack of energy. They have to adjust to a new world, every aspect of which is strange. You have to learn how to behave in your new role as the concerned, responsible, loving, but not primary, caregiver.

Choosing a Nursing Home

You may not have the luxury of making a choice. If your parent is too sick to return home but ready to leave the hospital, your selection of a nursing home is limited to whatever vacancy exists.

But if you do have some preparation time, some warning that your parent might need nursing home care, how do you decide which home to choose?

It is important, if at all possible, to include your parents in the decision to look for a nursing home. Occasionally, parents make the first move, saying that they feel more independent if they pay others to take care of them, or that they do not want to be a burden to their children. More often, you have to take the initiative and break the news that living at home is no longer a workable solution. Your parents are more likely to be accepting if they know the reasons. They may not like the outcome, but it is easier for them if they understand that you cannot give up your job or that their care is more than you can undertake. Honesty, however difficult, is always less hurtful than evasive lies.

By the time most parents need a nursing home, it is unlikely they can make the decision alone. Some talk about the move, a description of the home and its services, and, if possible, a visit will help them feel more respected and involved in a process that will affect them profoundly.

Nursing homes provide different levels of care, often within the same building. If you are uncertain about what kind of care is appropriate for your parents, a call to the admissions person, often the social worker, will help. That is your opportunity to hear about admission procedures, cost, and methods of payment, and any waiting list. By all means talk to anyone who personally knows any nursing home, especially those who have a relative living in one.

When selecting a nursing home, there is no substitute for a visit. If you have never been to a nursing home before, you may be shocked. Overwhelmed by the sight of large numbers of very old, disabled, and confused people, your immediate reaction may be to recoil, refusing to admit that this is a suitable place for your parent. You are reacting to your own feelings of grief and fear, however; your parent may not be as dismayed and may not feel so different from the other residents. If you can, see several nursing homes, and visit your favorite ones several times, at different times of day. Obviously it is important that they look and smell clean, that meals are attractively served, that the rooms are pleasant and that there is an activity program. But the most important component of a nursing home is the staff. They are a vital ingredient in the quality of your parents' lives. Only a visit allows you to see how the staff interact with the residents. Do they behave with respect and patience or appear harried? Are they are affectionate and pleasant or irritable and angry? Do they talk more to each other than to the people they are caring for? If possible, find out how long some of the staff have been there. Nursing homes sometimes have difficulty keeping their employees. Caring for chronically ill people is a demanding job and, in our society, not rewarded by money or status. Nevertheless, some administrators are able to make their staff feel valued and cared for, and they in turn create a comfortable, secure atmosphere for the residents.

Your parent has special needs, likes, and dislikes and you are in the best position to assess how a nursing home meets those needs. What makes a difference to your parent? Does the program include some activities they would enjoy? Many people with dementia spend a great deal of their day walking and become agitated if not able to do so. If this is true of your parent, it is worth checking how the staff handle this. Preferably there are places in and out of doors where residents can walk safely and without the need for constant supervision.

The location of the nursing home is important because this affects the number of visitors and frequency of visits. For your parent, it is likely to be more important to be close to one relative who will visit often than to be in aesthetically beautiful surroundings. Distance does count. Even with the best intentions in the world, it is difficult to make regular and frequent visits to your parents when the journey is long.

Visiting in a Nursing Home

Leaving Mom in the nursing home was one of the hardest things I'd ever done. She didn't belong there. All the residents looked so old and disabled; some were staring into space, others were walking aimlessly, one was moaning. I prayed she wouldn't be there long.

Mom did get a little stronger, but she still needs help getting in and out of bed, going to the bathroom, and dressing herself. Also, she's not as alert as she used to be. The doctor said her brain may have been damaged by the stroke.

I visit Mom every day on my way home from work. I stay until supper so that I can push her to the dining room and cut up her food before I leave. The staff are kind, but they don't have time to pay attention to small things. I do Mom's laundry and keep an eye on her clothes. I like to do something for her. Talking is difficult though. It's easier if we can go outside and look at the flowers. Or sometimes I can take in photographs of the family. Often, she's too tired to talk much at all and seems to prefer me to be quiet but stay with her.

Gradually I've come to see the nursing home in a new light. The residents, who at first had looked nothing but hopeless and decrepit to me are now individuals. Of course, I've gotten to know most of them by name, and some I always make a point of speaking to. At first, I was annoyed when someone wandered uninvited into Mom's room or interrupted us when we were talking, but I noticed that Mom was not upset. She seemed to have accepted that people behave differently here.

The role of the family is crucial in the lives of old people who live in nursing homes. It is clear from numerous studies and staff reports that people who have regular visitors adjust more quickly and happily to their new life. Nursing homes are set up to provide skilled physical care and supervision, and they are good at that, but you and your family still give the best emotional care, love, and sense of well-being.

You may wonder whether you should avoid visiting your parent for the first few weeks after admission, feeling that they need an undisturbed opportunity to get used to a strange place. Perhaps for some residents very frequent and lengthy visits add to their confusion and slow their adjustment to a new routine. For most, however, frequent visits help them to feel comfortable more quickly. When they see you, your parents may become upset, complain, cry, or even beg to be taken home. It is not easy. In all likelihood, you will feel acutely uncomfortable at seeing their distress. You will be tempted to stay away. But there are worse things than your parents getting upset, and feeling forgotten is one of them. They need to be able to grieve — grieve the loss of their home and independence — and to know that they are still part of your lives. For this to happen they need the presence of you and other people they love.

In addition to giving your emotional support, there are some practical ways you can help your parents adjust. You can accompany them to a meal, to an activity, and help them meet some of the other residents. Eventually, places, people, and routine will become familiar, but at first everything is strange. It is immensely reassuring during those first uneasy weeks for your parent to see a known, beloved face and to have an island of comfortable familiarity for a while. It helps if you recognize out loud that this move demands a huge adjustment on their part and that you will be as supportive as you can. "I know this is new and difficult for you, Mum, but I'll stick by you and help as much as possible."

If visits can be difficult, saying "goodbye" at the end of them is especially so. When your parents sense that you are about to leave, they may become more upset and clinging. Again, it helps to acknowledge that your parents have much to be sad about. But when it is time to leave, a firm affectionate goodbye with a reminder of the next visit gives a clear message that the nursing home is where they have to live, but that does not mean you have forgotten them.

The end of your visit means that your parents have to move from being with you to being without you in the nursing home. In the early weeks, this may be a desolate moment. They may have difficulty negotiating the transition. You can make it easier and, with it, your own leaving, by ensuring that your parents are not left feeling lost as you walk out of the door. If you ask, the staff may give them some special attention and find some way of distracting them. Or you can time your departure to coincide with an activity your parents enjoy — a meal, a television program.

You will probably find that visits gradually become easier as your parents adjust to life in the nursing home and accept that that is where they live. All of you settle into a pattern of when and how you spend time together. Each one of us needs to know that we have some relevance, and this is as true in old age as at any other. Old people need to know that they are part of the world and connected to their life before they came to the nursing home. You are the most important connection. Your very presence brings the world in, along with news of other family, neighbors, and acquaintances. Even if your parents are severely confused and cannot give you a name, they usually recognize you as someone who has some special meaning.

Although good nursing homes try to expand institutional life by organizing trips and outings, for most residents it is primarily their family that introduces variety. Visits home, a drive, a meal in a restaurant add pleasure and variety to the routine. If your parents cannot leave the nursing home, food cooked at home and brought in may be a treat. You may find it helpful to develop certain rituals or activities that become a focus for your visits. These may range from checking your parents' clothing, to reading or writing letters for them, to reading out loud. There is also value in predictable visits. If your parents can anticipate your visits, they may be happy for hours before you arrive. To know that something good is happening tomorrow makes today more enjoyable. If they are confused about time and forget that you always comes on a certain day, you may ask the staff to remind them.

If your parents become very sick and mentally incapacitated, their world shrinks to the size of the nursing home and the present moment. They are no longer able to show interest in the activities and happenings of other family members. With no awareness of the future or much of the past, conversation almost comes to a stop. Communication is no longer primarily verbal. Companionable silence, holding hands, smoothing on skin lotion, brushing hair may be more full of meaning than talk. It is the contact with beloved people that remains important.

You may discover that your relationships with your parents actually improve after they have moved to a nursing home. Removed from the pressures of daily care, it is easier for you to be affectionate and patient, and your parents may be calmer and more appreciative of you. Your visits are a time for being together with no other demand or expectation for that moment.

Another important role for you is as an advocate. Most frail older people cannot look out for themselves, and with the best organization in the world, nursing home staff sometimes fall short. You move from providing care yourself to ensuring that others do so. Your parents have a right to be respected and properly cared for. On the other hand, people's perception of neglect can come from many sources, only some of which originate with the staff. To unhappy people nothing is right. Any complaints your parents or other visitors make should be checked, but with an open mind as to whether they are justified or not. While it is important that you are actively concerned for your relatives' welfare, some families do place excessive demands on the staff, criticizing and interfering in their care. Nursing homes have their limitations. Frail people continue to deteriorate, the food does not please everyone, roommates can be difficult, and staff are too busy to be ideally attentive. On the other hand, some nursing homes do provide poor care and abuses do exist. If your concerns are justified and not corrected, you need to make official complaints, first to the administration and then, if necessary, to the state ombudsman or licensing authority.

In an ideal arrangement, you and the staff work as a team. They provide the day-to-day care, but you are the one who knows your parents' likes and dislikes, their interests and their past. It is a tragedy if old people lose their past just because there is no one around them who knows anything about them except their medical condition and which room they are now inhabiting. They are often unable to speak coherently about their past themselves or may assume that people are too busy to be interested. You can fill this vacuum by bringing in photographs and important possessions. If you tell the staff some of your parents' life story, they might then refer to children, grandchildren, work, and home towns.

Many family members who regularly visit nursing homes attest to the importance of knowing the staff who care for their relative and developing a good relationship with them. Similarly, staff enjoy having a positive relationship with the family of the residents under their care. The welfare of your parent then becomes a joint effort and benefits accordingly.

Legal Steps

People of all ages dread that they will become unable to manage their own affairs and make decisions about their lives. It is a frightening prospect to lose that control. Yet most of us will need someone else to attend to our affairs and make decisions on our behalf at some point in our lives. We may be incapacitated temporarily, as after surgery, or permanently, as in Alzheimer's disease.

The reality is that most of us will become permanently incompetent in the last days before we die. Medical science has progressed (if that is the right word in this context) to the point of prolonging physical life longer than the brain's ability to think clearly.

If your parents have not taken legal steps to control their finances and their medical care in the event that they become mentally incapacitated, it is worth encouraging them to do so. They should know that they can let their wishes be known while they are able to do so and that those wishes will be respected if they are unable to take part in any discussion.

Power of Attorney and Guardianship

The power of attorney is a legal document in which one person names another to help with his or her affairs. The document may specify certain rights, such as the signing of checks, or may be general and extensive. The person signing the document does not give up his or her rights but extends them to the person named. This is a voluntary agreement, can be signed only by those who understand what they are signing, and can be withdrawn at any time.

The durable power of attorney extends the agreement even after signers become incompetent. If your parents have a dementia, this document allows you to manage their affairs. Whenever the agreement comes into effect, and it may specify that it only applies if the signer becomes mentally incapacitated, it must be actually signed and witnessed while that person is competent.

Guardianship, on the other hand, is not a voluntary agreement. It is sought when a person is incompetent, unsafe, unable to manage his or her affairs, and refuses to allow others to do so. Full guardianship removes all of a person's legal rights as an adult and appoints someone else, usually a family member, as the guardian. Guardianship can be limited to specific areas, such as health care, financial affairs, appointing a guardian with power only in those matters. A petition for guardianship involves attorneys, a court hearing, and testimony from a doctor as to the subject's competence. It is an expensive and upsetting experience which, fortunately, can usually be avoided by obtaining a durable power of attorney when the person is competent.

Living Will

Most people dread the prospect of dying a prolonged death, hooked to machines in an intensive care unit. "I want to go quickly" is rarely a choice that can be made, however. Speeding our death is not much under our control. The living will helps to reduce the possibility that people's lives will be artificially prolonged beyond their wishes. Most states now recognize the right to refuse treatment under certain circumstances and the living will is an affirmation of a person's wish to assert that right. It sets out the grantor's requests about care in the event of becoming incurably ill, with no chance of recovery and unable to communicate at that time. It is usually limited to withholding or withdrawing treatment but, if desired, can contain clauses about withholding food and liquids if they have to be given by artificial means. Doctors, nursing homes, and family members should all have a copy.

Your parent may assure you that they have talked to their doctor about "no heroic measures" but a written document has power and certainty at times when both may be vital. In a hospital, with unknown doctors, you may need evidence of your relative's preferences for their care.

In many states, it is possible to grant a power of attorney for health affairs to a named person who can then make decisions about health care if the grantor becomes comatose or mentally incompetent. This carries more power and covers a wider range of contingencies than a living will alone.

If parents become terminally ill and unable to communicate and they left no prior direction, you have to fall back on what you think they would have wanted. You might be able to recall previous conversations with your parent about terminally ill friends or even pets that indicate their views. "They shouldn't have to suffer" or "Everything possible should be done." Such decisions are not only agonizing for you and your family to make, but you may disagree about what course of action to take. It is much easier if there is written evidence of what your parents want.

Points to Consider

1. Planning and forethought can be constructive and prevent potential difficulties.

2. If you are a caregiver, remember that it is important to take care of yourself too, and that includes holding reasonable expectations of yourself and using available help. Do not give up all friends and activities so that life narrows to caregiving.

3. If you are experiencing serious signs of stress, get some help. Talk to a therapist, find a support group, obtain more respite, take care of yourself.

4. Whatever arrangement you make, whether it is helping your parents in their own home or bringing them into yours, reassess periodically to check that it is still working for all of you.

5. Before your parents move in, discuss as many potential problems as possible — use of space, time together and separate, financial contributions, what each expects to give to and receive from the other.

6. Explore the feelings you have about nursing homes because they will influence your judgment and the decision you make.

7. If possible, visit possible nursing homes, looking at them with your parents' needs and likes in mind.

8. Get to know the staff who care for your parents. Housekeeping staff may be as important to your parents as the nurses. Try to foster a feeling of partnership with the staff with your parents' welfare being the common goal.

9. Encourage your parents to have some personal possessions in their room. Not only will they feel more comfortable, but photographs, cards, and pictures stimulate questions and conversation from the staff.

10. Deal with complaints, your parents' and your own, as objectively as possible. Have realistic expectations of the staff and do not get into power struggles unless you have good reason to do so.

11. If your parents have not signed a power of attorney (preferably durable power of attorney) and a living will, suggest that they do so. Consider doing the same yourself.

· Chapter 5 ·

What to Say

&

THE WORDS WE USE, and how we use them, are vital components of all our relationships. With words we try to convey what we know, think, feel, and, as we listen to words, we strive to understand the same of others. Important though words are, they are only part of communication. Our tone of voice, posture, and facial expression are among the many subtle cues that enrich and complicate the way we pass information to each other. Accurate, sensitive communication is both difficult and essential. It is hardly surprising that with the many signals we have to choose from, misunderstandings abound.

As your parents begin to fail and you are drawn more into their world, your ability to comprehend each other becomes extremely important. Without it, you cannot know what they worry about, want, or feel. In an effort to get things done, you may be tempted to bypass the time-consuming and often frustrating task of listening and go straight to problem solving. But if you fail to understand what your parents actually want and need, your plans, however sensible, may sour.

Few problems cannot be helped by good communication, and few cannot be made worse by the lack of it.

Jack often found it frustrating to try to help his parents.

This communication stuff is difficult. I'm not good at it — with my parents anyway. I worked hard to persuade them to move from their house — it was obvious to everyone else that it was too large. When something needs to be done, I don't see the point of debating it forever. But now I'm wondering if I was right. In every practical way they are better off — in a modern condo and near me — but they're miserable. Dad criticizes everything: the place is shoddily built, the grass isn't cut often enough. Mom misses her friends. I'm at a loss to know what they want, let alone what to do about it. I guess we've never been good at talking, but now it seems to matter more.

Listening

Listening is a much underrated skill in terms of both its value and its difficulty. Most of us assume that we are good listeners; most of us are wrong. All too often we let words wash over us, catching some of the content but little of the meaning that the person speaking to us is trying to convey. Our own reactions, associations, and intervening thoughts are often more compelling and may have little to do with what is being said. Listening is a challenge because it involves the work of actively trying to understand another human being.

With all its difficulties, listening is a skill worth working on. Of all tools, it is the one that enables us to discover what others are thinking and feeling. By listening, we create an opportunity to connect more deeply.

Looking back, I should have been suspicious when my parents weren't enthusiastic about my idea that they move. I was so sure that it was the right thing — and I still think it made sense under the circumstances. But I suppose I was too forceful. Would it have been better if I'd encouraged them to talk more — about what they wanted, various alternatives, what they'd have to give up? Chances are that they would have moved anyway, but Dad probably would feel different if he'd made the decision, and I certainly wouldn't feel as bad as I do right now.

Listening is not a passive activity. It requires active attention. Often the words *not* said are as important as those actually spoken. To understand what your parents mean, you have to be sensitive to the feeling behind their words. If they say something like "Children don't care about their parents any more," they may be making a general observation, but it is just as likely that they feel neglected by you. What they may be leaving unsaid is "You don't pay me as much attention as I'd like." If you listen carefully and undefensively, you will learn something about them and how they see the people and things around them.

Another thing that really worries me is the relationship between my mom and dad. He's always been a bit of a tyrant, but for the most part he kept his criticism for us kids. With Mom he was pretty respectful and affectionate. Now, perhaps because he only has her to boss, he's become so controlling of her. For instance, he quizzes her about what she's bought at the grocery store and complains bitterly if meals aren't on time.

Last week, for the first time I can remember, Mom let on that he could be difficult. My immediate reaction was that I'd talk to him and tell him he needed to straighten out. She was horrified and vetoed that idea fast. She's right. If I'd put my oar in, he'd have been so furious it would have made the situation worse. I didn't know what to say to Mom. Perhaps they should try counseling, but I knew the answer to that one before it was out of my mouth.

Because words are often a clumsy means for conveying the nuances of feeling, effective listening demands not only our effort and attention, but sometimes deciphering skills. Clues may be easily overlooked unless we are mindful of the complete context in which they are offered. Only too frequently you may try to guess what your parents want, leap in with your own suggestions, and, like Jack, are wrong as often as you are right. To have any chance of understanding, you have to be open-minded and suspend judgment. Otherwise, your replies may be irrelevant, ill-chosen, or in some other way fail to meet your parent's concerns.

Fortunately, there is time and room for correction. When your parent's expression or reply shows that you have missed your step, you can try again. "I guess I didn't really understand. Tell me more." "I've been thinking about our conversation last week and realize I didn't really answer you."

I really tried to stop offering advice and listened to Mom instead. Actually she wasn't asking for my opinion, but she said it helped her to vent about Dad sometimes.

I do see my father a little differently than I used to. Old age and retirement are hard for him. He's managed to feel important all his life, but it's not so easy now. He may be difficult at times, and that can get Mom down, but her philosophy is that when you have loved each other for fifty years, you put up with some bad times. It works for them, I guess.

Another problem with listening for most of us is that it does take time, and time is a commodity in short supply. Our perception of time varies over our life cycle. For young children it has no meaning, for older children it is unbounded, for adults it is frustratingly scarce. As someone with responsibilities pressing from all directions, you may want visits to your parents to be efficient, with a quick exchange of news, help with a necessary task, and settling of any decisions. To your parents, however, such visits may appear to be (as they sometimes are) a performance of a duty. They are ultimately unsatisfying to all concerned. Not that each visit can be a relaxed occasion, with time for tea and talk. But it is worth noting whether every contact with your parents is focused on tasks, with one eye on the clock and thoughts elsewhere. Are you making it impossible to have more than a brief conversation?

To find what is really going on for your parents, you need to slow down. In order to appreciate what is important to them, it helps to spend time together that is not taken up with a full agenda of chores. Change your pace if you can, and settle into your parents' rhythm. Let the conversation drift occasionally. You may notice some interesting things. For instance, you may talk to one parent much more than the other. In many families, the father has so long relied on his wife to be the communicator with the children that a one-to-one conversation with him is rare. Or you may learn that your parents are thinking a great deal about their childhoods and have recalled some details new to you, or that the flowers and birds in their garden are bringing them more pleasure as they become housebound. Their rich thoughts and experiences do not emerge in a short visit; they need time.

When you take the opportunity to listen to your parents, the interest and respect that you convey may be the most powerful message of all. Listening is a gift. If you have ever been a patient in a hospital, you may have felt neglected by the doctor who conducted an assessment of your progress from the doorway. You probably felt quite differently toward the doctor who came into the room and sat down. They may have spoken the same words and even stayed the same length of time, but your reaction was more positive to the second one. We convey similar messages in the way we converse with our parents.

How to Respond

Sometimes, listening is all that your parents need. They air their concerns and feel better. "A problem shared, is a problem halved," as my mother says. Sometimes listening is all we can do. Your parents' pain may have no solution, or at least none for the present, and the most caring thing you can do is sit and listen. And, sometimes, listening is the first vital step in dealing with a problem. By talking, your parents may come up with their own answers — answers they can then live with because they are their own. Jack was right in realizing that if he had let his parents reach their own decision, his father would probably have been more positive about his new home.

How and when to give advice is a sensitive issue. Any irritation that you and your parents feel for each other probably occurs around advice — the giving and taking (or not taking) of it. One of you gives it, the other resists or resents it.

The problem with most advice is that it is *our* solution to others' problems. When your parents complain or talk about a difficulty, you put yourself in their shoes, asking what you would do in their situation. However thoughtful you are, your answer may not be right for them. Jack thought that if his relationship with his wife was like his parents', then he would get help from a marriage counselor, but that was not an option they would consider. Make as many suggestions as make sense to you, but leave plenty of room for your parents to reach their own decisions.

Having grown up in an age that encourages self-awareness and openness, you may want your parents to talk more freely about their feelings. You may think they would be happier if they were in therapy, attended groups, or read certain books. Your parents have spent a lifetime handling their inner lives in their own way, however. While you may deplore their way, they are likely to feel confused and even criticized by your efforts to change them.

Your parents need time to consider your suggestions. They probably deliberate longer than you do before making their decisions. If they are not to feel harried, you have to be patient. If the solution seems obvious to you, why waste time discussing the pros and cons? Like Jack, you may think that your task is to direct your parents to the course of action that you see so clearly. In doing so you may imply that there is only one acceptable solution. At best, your parents could be mildly offended; at worst, they will yield to your opinion against their own inclinations.

It seems that we are often less likely to be patient or understanding with our family members than with those we know less well. Our arguments are often forceful and impatient. We want our loved ones to make good decisions, to be happy, and we are sure our answers are helpful.

If we are honest, how often has another person given us advice that we have taken, unless it confirmed our own wishes? Most of us need to make our own decisions. If this is true for you, you can be sure it is also true for your parents.

There are circumstances, however, in which your elderly parents want or need you to make their decisions. The reasons may be quite straightforward. They may have limited energy or expertise on certain matters and are relieved to have you take over the responsibility. Or they may be too sick or confused to make decisions about their own care.

There may be troubling reasons behind your parents' reliance on you. Parents who have never been comfortable making decisions alone are likely to turn to you when their spouse is no longer able to take charge. Others lose confidence in their own opinions, assuming that the younger generation knows best. Unfortunately, the negative stereotypes about old age are only too often held by the elderly themselves. They may be easily persuaded by people whom they assume to be better informed and more competent than they are. "I'll ask my son about whether I should sell my house; he'll know what I should do." "My doctor said I was killing myself and must put my husband in a nursing home." Still others may follow suggestions because they want to please the people who made them. Sons, daughters, doctors, lawyers may have useful information and opinions, but their youth or authority do not necessarily mean that their advice should be taken.

If you are asked for your advice, be clear that you are giving your opinion and that your parents need to come up with a decision in their own way.

Communicating with Confusion

If your parents have a dementing illness, such as Alzheimer's disease, you know that communication has become difficult. Depending on the stage of the disease, they probably struggle with words and may be unable to follow what you are saying. You will improve your chances of being understood if you speak slowly and use short, uncomplicated sentences. Minimize confusion by giving only one instruction or asking only one question at a time.

Your parents are probably aware that their brains are not functioning as well as they used to. They may say "I feel stupid" and become quite frustrated at their inability to express themselves. Rather than leave them to struggle, which makes them more anxious, it is often a help to suggest a word to fill in the blank. Your tone of voice makes all the difference. If you are snappy or impatient, your parents are likely to become tense or irritated. Conversely, if you can be warm and respectful, they usually feel less inadequate and behave more calmly.

If your parents' efforts to communicate remain unsuccessful — and that often happens however hard you both try — and you see your parent growing agitated, then try changing the subject or suggest doing something different until the agitation passes.

In the later stages of a dementia, your parents' language may appear to make no sense at all. Sentences begin coherently, only to tail off into silence or non-sequiturs. Words are garbled into nonsense. Comments may be spoken clearly but bear no relation to anything going on. If you listen carefully, you may be able to pick up a clue of what your parents are trying to communicate. For instance, "Where is my mother?" may indicate that your parent is feeling bereft and needs comfort. "I want everyone out of here" may not be hostile but a signal that the surroundings are too confusing and some quiet is needed. When language is badly deteriorated, interpretation may require an act of imagination on your part. You may guess incorrectly, but if your voice is patient and interested, your parents can sense that you are on their side and taking them seriously. The subtle cues of nonverbal communication become more and more important often with effective and satisfying results for both of you.

When Problems Occur

I don't like to admit this, but I find it hard to visit my parents. I do it — I try to pop in once a week on my way home from work — but it's an obligation, not a pleasure. But they really expect these visits. I sometimes have the feeling that they have been sitting, not moving, since my last visit. I always leave with a sense of dissatisfaction. The three of us really don't have much to say to each other. I wonder if they find the conversation as awkward as I do.

With my father, it's worse than uncomfortable. It seems to me that we've not been able to agree on anything since I was a teenager. He's so set in his opinions, and he's always right. Even my job — I'm a teacher — is no way to earn a decent living if you're a man with a family. He can't stop pointing it out at every available opportunity. I do try not to get drawn into an argument, but he knows how to touch my sore spots, and I end up defending myself again. I'd like to handle these conversations differently. I end feeling criticized and angry, Mom gets tense, my wife has to put up with my bad mood, and I can't believe my father is happy either.

It may be a source of wonder and annoyance as you watch your-self slip back into younger ways of behaving as you step over the threshold into your parents' house. Despite your good intentions, old feelings and patterns of behavior intrude, making visits with your parents awkward or even painful. And your parents probably con-tribute to your slide. Failing to remember that you are a responsible adult, they may continue to hand out advice and judgment in a way that they would not with any other adult. In one support group, a member who had been listening to others' struggles, suggested that they all trade parents. Her point was that the feelings and shared history make it difficult to deal with problems in their own families. One woman who successfully managed a staff of fifteen people could not contemplate talking to her father about his alcoholism. Child-hood fears and emotional ties compound the difficulty of resolving problems.

Your reactions to your parents may be automatic, grounded in long years of practice. Just as Jack repeatedly responded defensively to his father's critical comments about his job, you may persist in doing the same thing time and time again, knowing what the result will be. You argue, drop hints, reason, become angry, all of which you have tried many times before without success. When you are stuck in an unproductive and unsatisfying pattern, there is one thing you know for certain: your usual way of doing things is not work-ing. It is time to try something new. Not that it is easy. Habit, fear, lethargy, all conspire to make change difficult. It is *you* that you have to change, and we all find that much harder to do than to say.

The first step to change is to recognize that it does take two to argue. Your parents say something that triggers off a negative emo-tional response in you. You then reply in a way that sets off an emotional response in your parents, and a heated argument or re-sentful withdrawal ensues. The circle can be broken at any point. It can be broken by either of you; your parents can choose to respond differently, and so can you.

If you want to, you can prevent a quarrel from ever happen-ing. You can refuse to be drawn in, change the subject, even leave the room when you see an argument approaching. One powerful response to a critical comment is to agree with it. Then there is noth-ing to fight about. Jack realized that his father's negative judgments about his work had some truth in them. Had they been voiced by a colleague or his wife, Jack would probably have agreed that teaching was not a well-paid profession, nor one that carried much status. By joining with, instead of opposing, what his father was saying, Jack could create the opportunity for a different interaction. One of my clients dreaded her visits with her mother because she invariably felt criticized and put down by her. A typical greeting from her mother was "You've put on weight." After the daughter learned to respond with "Yes, you're right," or "Do you think so?" a subtle but important change took place. Her mother was not getting the response she wanted and rapidly lost interest in that particular remark. The daughter felt stronger as she moved from a position in which she reacted as a vulnerable child to that of an autonomous adult.

You may be able to encourage your parents to change by telling them directly how you react to certain comments or actions on their part. Parents rarely choose to have an uncomfortable relationship with their children, but they may be at a loss to know how to behave any differently. If advice, criticism, lecturing has been their style, they may continue to relate in that way. It is a common misconception that elderly people cannot change. That belief, in itself, is a barrier to communication. It is worth giving your parents the benefit of the doubt. When you feel unappreciated or unsupported, gently let your parents know how you feel. The result may be a welcome surprise. You may be telling them something that they did not realize, and that they may try to correct. While we cannot force others to change, we can provide opportunities for them to alter their own behavior. It may not work, but it is worth trying.

When confronting others about something they have done or said, it is very helpful to use "I" messages. By this I mean, speaking in terms of how "*I* feel," avoiding the use of "*you.*" For example, "I feel put in the middle when you find fault with my wife," rather than "You always complain about my wife." "I" messages are powerful because they avoid blaming. They are also honest and difficult to argue with. A mother can hardly argue with her son's feeling about being put in the middle, but she is likely to react defensively to the accusation that she always puts him in the middle. The chance of a positive change is much greater if people do not feel blamed or accused.

Most change, either in our parents or ourselves, is slow and limited. There are powerful forces pulling us back into our familiar ways of behaving. Jack, for example, found that he was only partially successful in having conversations with his father. It was all too easy to be drawn back into an argument. His father threw out negative comments and Jack eventually took the bait. Persistence has its reward, however. If you consistently respond in a calm, direct manner, your message will eventually be clear to yourself and your parents.

Good communication does not guarantee that you agree with each other. You and your parents may have difficulty tolerating that you do not always hold similar opinions or even see each others' point of view. You want your parents to understand you, and they often react as if your behavior is a reflection on them even though you have reached middle age. One of my clients felt such personal shame that her favorite granddaughter was living with a man she had not married that she was unable to tell the truth to her friends. She was so upset that she could not see her granddaughter without expressing her disapproval and disgust. Not surprisingly, her granddaughter was angry and stopped visiting her. Fortunately, the two of them recognized that their relationship was too important to lose. They were never going to live by each other's values, but they could agree not to agree and accept their differences. If you and your parents can have open discussions, you may be able to differ without animosity and, over time, perhaps even appreciate the other's position.

Some of your parents' comments may have no satisfactory answer and no acceptable solution. You have to settle for trying to understand your parents' feelings and not making a painful situation worse. If your mother is unhappy to be in a nursing home and repeatedly asks you to take her home, you might respond: "I don't blame you. I'd be unhappy too if I were here and not in my own home." She may or may not be appeased, but at least she knows she is heard and understood.

Nonverbal Communication and Touch

The words we use are only one of the ways we communicate with each other. Our tone of voice, facial expression, position of our body, all say a good deal, and say it powerfully. If the expression on our face disagrees with the words we speak, it is our face that makes the greater impression. If a son-in-law says to his wife's mother, "I didn't know you were staying the night" and speaks lightly, with a smile, she will probably take his words as affectionate teasing, but if he has a frown and a serious tone, she will certainly get a message that she is unwelcome. It is a testimony to the power of nonverbal communication that it takes me many written words to try to explain something that would be instantly obvious if we were talking face to face.

If your parents have a dementia, your words have become less important than your mood and tone of voice. They may not comprehend what you say but are quick to react to, and reflect, your manner, whether you are calm, irritable, impatient, or good humored.

Touch is important to us, and yet we pay scant attention to it, until we are without it. Of all the senses it is the one best able to comfort. One of the sorrows of old people, especially for those who live alone, is that they are touched very little. It is not surprising if they delight in very young children who like to be held and hugged. Touch can convey so much — reassurance, concern, affection — and often more efficiently than words. If your parents have lost the ability to see, hear, talk, or understand speech, touch may become the most effective way to communicate. Sometimes it is the only way. When other senses have lost their efficacy, a hug, holding hands, a touch on the shoulder lets your parents know that they are loved.

Humor

Humor is the leavening force in all human interaction. Even our most serious disagreements seem less earth-shaking if we can retain some capacity to laugh at ourselves or our situation.

Humor makes it easier to say difficult things and also to hear them. Your parents may be able to be gently teased about characteristics that you find irritating, such as their tendency to treat you like children or their refusal to give up on a particular piece of advice. If you speak with gentle humor, you can make a point in a way that rarely causes an upset. Humor has an intimacy when it is genuine and considerate. It is destructive and unfair, however, to turn it into something that hurts, as with sarcasm. Your tone of voice is often the difference between humor and hurt. For your part, remember to react as you would like your parents to react. Be slow to take offense. There is no virtue in being sensitive to every comment, choosing to see your parents as thoughtless and controlling. Even if they are being unfair, it is wise to let many negative comments slide.

If you can keep your sense of humor, you will help your parents carry the frustrations, and even the embarrassments that come with aging, more lightly. Their losses, whether memory, stamina, or continence, acquire a disproportionate importance if you all pretend that they are not happening and collude in a cover-up. An obvious memory lapse that both you and your parents try not to notice can be more awkward than a light comment or even teasing about "your forgettery is in fine form today."

If your parents are frail and confused, you may sometimes feel heartbroken as you watch their mistakes and struggles. Faced with both pain of deterioration and a muddle in which you can see some comedy, humor can be the balm that soothes both of you. One woman at a loss to know how to respond to her husband's hundredth assertion that he was going to live with his long-dead mother, finally said, "Fine, but take the shovel." She felt better and he temporarily was content to let the subject drop.

Typically, there is much laughter in meetings of support groups as members recognize the amusing and even ridiculous situations in which they all find themselves. Their humor is a gift that eases the burden of caregiving. Without it, the pain would be unbearable.

What to Talk About

I'm doing better with my father. We don't get into as many arguments now that I'm less defensive and edgy with him. But we still don't have much to say to each other. Perhaps even less now that we don't fight! It's easier with Mom; it always has been. But even with her, when we've exhausted the subject of what the kids are doing, we lapse into silence. It's amazing how different it is when my wife is with me. She and my mother find it easy to chat about all sorts of things. My wife knows much more about my mother's life than I do. And with my father, she's more relaxed than I am. She's the only person who can tease him. I don't know how she does it, but the atmosphere is certainly easier.

Most parents like to be included in your life. Indeed, you and your family's doings may make up a large proportion of their conversation with each other and their acquaintances. They like to know the details, not just the bare bones, of what is going on.

One subject that most older people enjoy talking about is the past, especially their personal past. Since their past is also yours, this may be enjoyable for you. Even if you have heard a story many times before, by listening and asking questions, you may hear details you have not heard before. Think of including your children, who may be genuinely interested in their grandparents' experiences. Many people who work with the elderly believe that reminiscence has a value in its own right. The gerontologist Robert Butler called this "life review." By looking back over their lives, especially in the company of someone who is interested, old people can derive a sense of satisfaction and accomplishment.

The most important things to say to your parents may be the easiest to overlook. If you love your parents, appreciate something they have done, value who they are, it is important to let them know that. One of my clients was moved and delighted when her daughter told her how much she treasured their friendship. "I guess I knew that," she said, "but it was wonderful to hear her say it." We so often assume that people know that we value them. They may not. In any case, expressions of love bear repeating frequently. It is important that we speak of our affection to anyone we are fond of, but for your elderly parents it carries a special weight and poignancy.

Difficult Subjects

"Should I let them know about my problems?" This is a question that I am often asked. How much to share difficulties varies from family to family and parent to parent. Your parents may react so strongly to your problems that they become preoccupied and sleepless. Others worry but prefer to be included: and indeed may feel patronized and left out if they are protected from painful issues. They want to be involved but increasingly, as they age, need to know that you can deal with your difficulties. On your side, you have to decide what is it like for you to talk to them about your problems. Do you value your parents' support, or are you inclined to keep your difficulties to yourself? How much to share is a personal judgment based on what you know of your parents, how you see them react, and your own preference. Do they become overly anxious? Do they enjoy being asked for their advice? Are they able to listen to you and be supportive?

There are a number of topics that you would probably prefer not to talk about. Financial and legal arrangements, dying, and death are frequently among them. Sometimes your parents want to avoid facing these issues; more often, you do. Think about it. What might happen if your parents are no longer able to live alone? Do your parents have wishes about the distribution of their belongings after they have died? Where and how do they want to be buried or cremated? Such matters are never easy to talk about but are less difficult to discuss before the problem becomes urgent.

Many older people have reported to me that they have opened the subject of "when I am gone," only to have their children dismiss the subject with comments like "Don't talk that way," or "You'll be here for ages yet." Most older people are not afraid of death, though they often have fears about the process and, in particular, dread being dependent on others before death actually comes. It is important to them that they leave their affairs in good order.

Rarely, however, do parents take the initiative to sit down with their family and tell them of their wishes for the handling of their belongings, their final illness, and their funeral. Now that medical science can keep our bodies alive long after we have lost awareness, it is important for all of us to consider our preferences about our own dying and let others know while we are still able to do so. The death of your parents is upsetting enough without the additional difficulty of guessing after the fact what they would want and then sorting it out with the rest of your family. It helps to have discussed these matters beforehand. That will not only make the handling of your parents' deaths less traumatic, but also helps them have some sense of order and control over the last stage of their lives.

Most parents make occasional comments or hints, such as "When I go, I hope I go fast," or "I won't always be here you know," or "I don't want to be dependent on you children." If you listen, you will hear many such statements. Your parents are giving you an opportunity to pick up on subjects that they think about often — nursing home, dying, disposal of assets — but avoid discussing openly because it is painful for everyone.

Propelled by love, guilt, or a sense of duty, you may make specific promises to your parents about the future. A common one is "I will never let you go into a nursing home." Unfortunately, none of us can predict the future. You may make a promise that you cannot ultimately keep. It is wiser and more honest to say that you will do the best you can and will not abandon them.

If your parents do not open the subject of arrangements for the end of their life, it is up to you to do so. How do you raise topics if your parents do not give openings? Straightforwardness is the best policy. Your discussion is more likely to be fruitful if you choose the time with care, even taking the step of setting the scene ahead by warning them that you have something important to talk about. You might try introducing the topic in a letter, giving them time to think without needing an immediate response. Or you may find it easier to initiate the subject by mentioning something you read in the paper or heard on the news. "I read about the new living will legislation; have you thought of making one for yourself?" "I've been thinking about making a will for myself; have you done anything about that?" Your parents may be more receptive if you speak in terms of the effect on you. "I worry about you." "It will be easier for us if you let us know what you want."

Difficult topics are rarely aired and resolved quickly. Do not be in a rush to have decisions made. These are heavy matters for your parents. They need time to consider, react, and come up with questions before they have answers. Sometimes it may seem to you that they did not hear you only to find later that they had been doing some serious thinking. On a recent visit to my parents, I mentioned that I had made a living will and wondered what they would want if they become terminally ill and unable to make their own decisions. They were interested but noncommittal and, to my disappointment, the subject was dropped. Two weeks later, they told me that they had been to their favorite beach and spent the afternoon talking about their deaths. They had thought that they knew each other's wishes, only to find that there were some things they had never explicitly talked about.

On the other hand, your parents may never mention the topic you carefully raised, leaving you with the dilemma of whether to bring it up again. After two attempts, you have to let most subjects drop. Your parents may have dealt with it in their own way and not told you, or are not ready to face it. You have done as much as you can at present.

If dying is difficult enough to talk about when it is in the presumably distant future, it is much more so when it is imminent. Yet, to avoid the subject when your parents are terminally ill is similar to not talking about the proverbial elephant in the living room. You are all thinking about the one thing you are not mentioning.

Of all topics, death is one we most seek to avoid. We are afraid of causing our loved ones pain and of feeling it ourselves. Yet loneliness is a greater pain. When I ask elderly people what they most fear about dying, "being alone" is at or close to the top of the list. Dying is a big unknown, and we want the love and support of those dear to us as we approach it.

As with all difficult subjects, it is important to be sensitive and pick up on any cues your parents give. Comments such as "I don't think I'm going to get better this time," or "Will you look after your mother?" indicate an openness to talk. To protect yourselves from pain, it is tempting to offer quick reassurance — reassurance that is false: "You've beaten the odds before. I'm sure you'll do it again." The elephant is in the living room, but not mentioned. To follow up on leads may open a discussion that brings a comfort to you both. To ignore them risks your relationship becoming superficial and careful. If you should get such cues from your parents, convey that you are there and listening. If they are beyond talk, a squeeze of your hand may convey your presence and understanding more eloquently than any words. If they can talk, ask questions and encourage them to air their feelings and thoughts. It will soon become clear that fears are fed by silence; good, open communication is the only real antidote.

When your parents are sick, they probably prefer to be told the truth about what is wrong with them. They want to know what to expect, even if that is death — to be given some reassurance of help and support until the end. For most people, fantasy, uncertainty, and anxiety are harder to endure than the truth. Unless they insist that they do not want to know, your parents should be given the facts. Telling them that they are dying is excruciatingly painful for you and your family, and even the professionals involved, but they should not be denied the opportunity to put their affairs in order, to make special requests, to give last messages.

If your parents give no indication that they want to talk and do not pick up on your questions or hints that you want to do so, you can continue to listen carefully and keep the door open by affirming your willingness to listen if they want to talk. Your parents will probably die as they lived. Some will speak about their feelings, some not; some will deny they are dying, others face it with equanimity; some will be angry and resentful, others ready; some will be frightened, others comforted by the prospect of an afterlife.

Even if your parents are dying, you can help them live for the remainder of their days. They may be able to appreciate jokes and news about the family. They may want to hear about the plants in their garden or your golf game. Though you are painfully aware that they will not see another spring or swing a club again, you are helping them feel in touch with the world they know.

When the time for talk is past, companionship and touch remain. Your parents may seem barely aware of you, but there is enough evidence from people who have recovered from near-death experiences to believe that your loved ones sense your presence and love until their end.

Points to Consider

1. Before all, learn to listen. Pay attention to what your parents are not saying as well as what they are saying. Strive to understand what they are feeling beyond their words.

2. Be careful about how you give advice. It is important that your parents make their own decisions as far as that is possible. If they are unable to do so, try to help them feel part of the process.

3. When communication with your parents seems to be stuck in a rut, try changing your reaction. While you cannot change your parents' behavior, sometimes a small change on your part can lead to a positive shift.

4. Use "I" messages when confronting your parents, or anyone else.

5. Old people are often touch deprived. Touch is an effective way of conveying affection and giving comfort.

6. Try to keep a sense of humor. It will make any situation more tolerable.

7. On many topics, you and your parents may not agree with each other, but you can respect their opinions.

8. Most parents like to know what is going on in their family's lives and do not want to be left out of the problems. They want the opportunity to advise and be supportive but not to feel responsible.

9. Encourage your parents to talk about their deaths — the arrangements, their wishes, their fears.

· Chapter 6 ·

Sibling Rivalry and Other Family Relationships

❧

WHEN YOUR PARENT becomes frail or elderly your whole family is affected — your spouse and children, but especially you and your brothers and sisters. You are called upon to cooperate in a way that you may never have done before. Everyone is involved. Some take major responsibility, some offer help, advice, or criticism, some maintain an uncomfortable distance. Many families rally to the occasion, growing closer as they work together, whereas others find the demands so intolerable that they move farther apart. Faced with the necessity of making complicated decisions, you may be surprised to see old issues and feelings affect the way you think and communicate with each other. Needless to say, long-standing feelings of affection and loyalty make collaboration easier whereas old jealousies and lack of respect certainly make it more difficult.

Nowhere do these old feelings run more strongly than in the relationships between brothers and sisters.

Sometimes I wish I were an only child.

Pat was talking to the other members of a support group that met at the nursing home where her mother was a new resident. Jack had just complained that he had no brothers and sisters to share the responsibility of his father.

I don't really mean that but my brother and sister aren't much help. In fact when my sister decides to take an interest in Mom she makes trouble. For example, she just phoned to tell me to instruct the staff here to walk my mother at least twice a day. This is typical of the way she interferes. I'm the one who's cared for

107

Mom for years, but she acts the expert who is only too free with her advice.

Feelings between brothers and sisters can create tensions and resentments that not only seriously impede any attempts to cooperate around the care of a parent but cause ripples and rifts in relationships throughout the family. Once you recognize them, however, you have a chance of minimizing their damaging effects and even resolving them to create more positive relationships.

Family Patterns

The bond between you and you brothers and sisters is one of the longest-lasting of all human relationships, often extending for seventy years or more. You share the same parents and are exposed to similar values, expectations, and models of how to behave. The connection is not always a close one, however, and after adolescence, you have considerable choice about the amount of time and intimacy you share with each other. You may have a close friendship that you maintain over long periods and long distances. Or you may have little to do with each other. You are not obliged to get together except for family gatherings and, like Pat and her siblings, can elect to keep those contacts superficial.

I guess we get on as well as most families. My brother, Tom, and I were quite close as kids, but we never talk about anything heavy or personal. I've never told him, for instance, that my husband is often out of work in the winter and we worry about paying bills. Judy and I have nothing in common; you'd never know we were sisters, we're so different.

The past is a powerful influence. Many adult children cannot ignore old feelings and patterns of behavior even when meetings are brief and infrequent. The seeds sown in childhood lay dormant, ready to sprout whenever conditions are right. Conditions are prime when you and your siblings have to make a joint decision. Planning a combined gift or surprise celebration for your parents may provide a major challenge. The preparations can take on the air of a summit conference with covert fears and assumptions being more relevant than the stated agenda. Whose idea carries the most weight? Who supports whom? Who feels left out or burdened by an unfair share of the work?

Sibling rivalry has a long history, starting as it does when each young child's desire to be the center of the universe is confounded by brothers and sisters each vying for their parents' love and attention. Though the feelings lose some of their power over time and may disappear for long periods, they frequently reappear with an intensity that is often surprising.

My sister, Judy, is the one I have problems with. When we were kids, Tom and I called her bossy and she still is. She doesn't live far away — only two hours — but she is always too busy to visit Mom. And when she does come, she's a whirlwind, full of suggestions and strong opinions about what someone else should do. I've never been able to stand up to her. I bite my tongue until she leaves and then breathe a sigh of relief. I do talk to Tom sometimes — in fact I run up phone bills complaining about Judy — but there's nothing he can do. He's intimidated by her too. Actually I think he's relieved he lives so far away. He can only get here about twice a year, so he has every excuse for staying disconnected.

Family roles and identities have in part been defined by your parents and partly by yourselves in relation to your siblings: "She's the pretty one"; "He's the athletic one"; "She's the responsible one." Trained by many years of living together, you react to each other in certain prescribed ways. You all know who has the strongest voice, who needs protecting from unpleasant news, who is the favorite, the decision-maker. Your expectations are powerful though not always fully conscious and rarely spoken out loud.

Labels and family themes that might have had validity earlier in life do not always continue to apply in adulthood. Personalities and circumstances do change. Nevertheless, in times of emotional stress, we inevitably fall back on familiar patterns, acting as if they are reliable. An old shoe is more comfortable than a new one.

Unfortunately, old shoes sometimes leak. Among siblings involved in the care of their parents the leaks usually occur around the uneven division of work and responsibility. The role each of you plays depends on many factors, some of which have little to do with the task at hand. This is the pitfall of family labels. You may be identified as caregiver because you live close to your parents, are the oldest daughter, are unmarried, or are perceived as your parents' favorite. Some of these characteristics may have little to do with your ability or capacity to care for your parents. The oldest daughter may be expected to do much more for her parents than her brother who also lives nearby, despite the fact that she too has a full-time job, a spouse, and children. A son may be identified as the one to handle parents' finances, although he has little interest and less ability in this area than his sister. An unmarried daughter may be seen by her siblings as having plenty of opportunities to provide help, whereas she sees her time as a precious commodity if she is to have a personal life.

It is generally true that the most damaging situation occurs when expectations are based on perceived favoritism. Siblings may then abdicate responsibilities by placing them on one brother or sister because that child seemed favored.

Tasks are more likely to be appropriately distributed if each of you pays attention to the others' real capabilities. Family meetings can be invaluable in working out what needs to be done and by whom. So often, siblings talk in pairs rather than as a group, sharing some information, withholding some, scapegoating, and splitting into factions. They may pay more attention to complaining about each other than working on what their parents need. With all of you in one room at the same time, everyone hears the same opinions, information, and possible solutions. This openness increases the chance of solving problems. Where your family relationships are fragile, however, and especially if potentially explosive, such meetings may be destructive, and you and your siblings may need to work with each other individually. A professional, such as a social worker or psychologist, can be a useful consultant and possible facilitator of meetings.

The reality is that the distribution of responsibility among the siblings is unlikely to be equitable. How much each person takes on is largely determined by circumstances and often by physical location. If all of you can recognize the heavier load one is carrying, however, the primary caregiver is less likely to feel resentful and the others more sensitive about helping where possible.

I've always been closer to my mom than my brother and sister — perhaps because I'm the youngest, perhaps because my mom was widowed when I was only fourteen years old. Mom never dated or had much of a social life so we were together a lot, especially after Judy and Tom left home. I stayed around. My husband is local too, so we had no reason to move away.

Mom and I really were each other's best friend. We talked every day and there was hardly anything we didn't share. For many years Mom helped me a lot. You know the kind of thing — she'd mind the kids if I was held up at work, or pick up some things for me from the store. A few years ago though, things began to change. First, her arthritis made it difficult for her to get around. But the worst was her forgetfulness. I remember coming home one day to find my daughter out on the street trying to ride her older brother's bicycle and my mother dozing in the living room. She'd forgotten that the children were there.

Since then I've had to do more and more for her. First of all, I took over her shopping and cooked some meals because, left to her own devices, she just opened a can of soup. But before long that wasn't enough.

Families create their own balance — a balance of closeness, distance, power, responsibility. As with any balance, a change on one side will be felt on the other. Individually, we are complex creatures; families are even more complicated. The repercussions of any shift in relationships will often be far-reaching and unpredictable.

Change takes many forms. Some changes appear to be minor, such as one member deciding not to join the rest of the family for Thanksgiving. Others come as a crisis, such as a parent suffering a stroke; still others evolve slowly, as in a parent's gradual but disabling memory loss. Whatever form change takes in your family, it will be felt by all of you. You will be forced to adjust your habits and customs accordingly. It is at these times that emotional distance and balance are not easy to maintain.

While it is a rare family that has no resentments or jealousies, rarer still is a family that can talk constructively about these feelings. Children and adolescents deal with their differences within their family in a variety of ways. They quarrel, fight, endure silently, or ignore according to their personality, position within the hierarchy, or family custom. Parents also have their own styles. They may have been despots, benevolent dictators, or democratic leaders but, in their own way, they were usually there to mediate family differences. Even into adulthood, this role often continues, with parents acting as the link between the various members. When a parent becomes sick or less capable, these patterns change and children find themselves discussing difficult issues directly with each other without experience or a guide on how to do so. The manual or tools for problem-solving do not exist. Usually one child takes over the coordinator role, but there is a period of flux and reorganization before the new pattern is established.

Looking back, I realize we hadn't a clue how to talk to each other about what was going on with Mom. We couldn't even discuss small issues. I remember one year when I decided to have Thanks-

giving at my house because it was really too much for Mom. What a hornet's nest. Judy said if we were to change our usual arrangements, we must go to her house, which she considered more suitable than mine. Tom was not about to drive the extra miles to Judy's home and thought he wouldn't come at all. So we went back to our traditional Thanksgiving at Mom's house but with me doing all the work and pretending that Mom was more capable than she was. But of course we'd just postponed yet another discussion that would have to take place sooner or later.

I have to take some responsibility for our failure to communicate because I was certainly reluctant to be the bad guy and tell Tom and Judy what was really going on with Mom. To be honest, I didn't tell them much at all. Perhaps it would have been different if I'd seen them more often, but as it was we didn't even talk on the phone often. They telephoned Mom regularly, but I know she didn't tell them of her difficulties. Also there was always this unspoken agreement to make Tom and Judy's trips home pleasant and relaxed. They didn't come often, so Mom always made their visits into a celebration with special meals and so on. I seem to have kept that tradition going. Heaven forbid that I should raise any problem to spoil the atmosphere.

I did try talking to Tom when I first realized Mom was beginning to have trouble, but he completely brushed my concerns aside. He said things like, "Perhaps Mom is a bit depressed, but it'll pass," and "All older people have trouble with their memories but manage all right." I was a little angry with him but also relieved because I wanted to believe he was right, that I was fussing unnecessarily.

Most of us are reluctant to face problems that have not yet occurred. Issues are less painful, however, while they are at the "potential" stage. When people can talk about future scenarios, they may generate ideas and solutions, or at least begin a useful habit of joint discussion and decision-making. Most decisions cannot be made ahead of time. As parents grow old, almost everything — length of life, health, need for care — is an unknown. This is one of the things that makes planning impossible. A preliminary look at possible outcomes, however, will aid the process when decisions become necessary.

To broach the subject of your parents' old age is difficult, but if you and your family have brainstormed alternatives, you will be better prepared emotionally and practically.

Different Perceptions

One of the difficulties Tom, Judy, and I had was that we saw Mom differently. Consequently, we couldn't agree on what was best for her. This became very obvious when we finally sat down together to talk about her situation. We were forced into doing something by two crises that occurred in the same week. A neighbor called to report that she'd found Mom outdoors late one chilly evening, without a coat on and apparently not sure where she was. Then the fire alarm in the senior housing complex where she lived was triggered by an empty pot burning on her stove. The housing manager was kind enough but made it very clear that Mom was becoming a danger to the other residents.

Well, I don't know what I expected from our meeting, but it was a disaster. Tom, who seemed to be in a state of shock, withdrew from the discussion altogether, saying Judy and I should make the decisions because he couldn't think constructively. Judy was her usual outspoken self but contributed little beyond dogmatic pronouncements. She thought Mom could attend the Senior Center during the day and we could employ someone to cover the evenings. I had given a lot of thought to my mother's situation. I knew Mom was far too shy to be comfortable with a group of strangers, and she'd never understand why someone else was in her house. Judy's response was that Mom would have to learn a new way of doing things. I talked things over with my husband. Though our house would be crowded, we decided to take Mom in. I could hear the other two breathe a big sigh of relief, though Judy couldn't refrain from muttering something about us overreacting.

Just as no parents treat each of their children alike, so do siblings view their parents very differently. Indeed when discussing your parents, you and your brothers and sisters may sometimes wonder if you are talking about the same people. One son may see his mother as home-loving and nurturing, whereas another may see her as passive and dependent; a daughter may see her father as proud and independent, while another sees him as obstinate and manipulative. The way each of you perceives your parent is largely determined by your personality and your past experiences with your parent. Because of your differences, you and your siblings may view your parent's refusal to wear a hearing aid, for example, as obstinacy, as vanity, as an understandable reluctance to face the losses of old age, or as a natural but temporary adjustment to something new and unpleasant.

These differing viewpoints are important factors in any discussion and account for much of the disagreement that occurs. Add to that contrasting beliefs you hold about people's ability to change, individuals' right to determine their own lifestyles, and it is surprising that agreement is reached as often as it is.

Your siblings' opinions, though different from your own, usually have some validity. In all probability, not one of you is entirely right or wrong. If your parents are not able to let you know what they would like to happen, you have to rely on your own knowledge of what they need and what makes them comfortable. By listening to each other, you and your brothers and sisters may not only learn something useful, but also create an atmosphere in which you can work together.

> *I know Mom better than the others so I felt strongly about what we should do. Perhaps it's because I'm shy too, but I understand Mom's need for privacy and her reluctance to be much involved with people outside the family. Judy couldn't appreciate that at all. She was impatient with what she labeled as Mom's dependency and inability to change. Tom, on the other hand, couldn't acknowledge that Mom had deteriorated at all. He'd always seen her as strong and capable and he wouldn't see any different.*
>
> *Rather than quarrel with Tom and Judy, my husband and I went ahead and moved Mom in with us.*

Another hindrance to clear thinking among siblings is that each has an image to maintain, an image created over many years of living together. Judy's view of herself as the sister in charge clearly interfered with her capacity to work with the others, Tom's emotional distance rendered him useless, and Pat's habit of always accommodating to differing opinions restricted her ability to be honest about her mother's condition. You may have adopted the role of peacemaker, follower, or decision-maker. Without thinking about it, you stay in this role; it is comfortable because familiar. But, circumstances change, and you change. It is worth stepping aside occasionally to look at the situation with fresh eyes. Judy, for example, might have allowed herself to recognize that Pat was no longer the less experienced younger sister but had knowledge that could help them all as they considered their mother's situation. And Pat could have given herself credit for having useful information that she did not have to hide because it was unwelcome.

Sibling at a Distance

If you live far from your family you face special challenges. While physical distance and emotional distance are not the same thing and children who live at a considerable distance do have close relationships with their parents and siblings, intimacy under those circumstances does take some work, money, and effort.

When your parents become frail and need help, distance becomes more of a problem. Most of the practical chores, by necessity, fall to the siblings nearby. Relationships between those of you who can visit only occasionally and those involved with your parents on a daily basis may take on a new and potentially stressful dimension. The brothers or sisters who carry most of the responsibility may feel that the others are not pulling their weight. As the one living at a distance you may feel uncertain about how to help or left out of the information and decision circuit.

> *I suppose it's not easy for Tom and Judy either. I'm not very good at letting them know how they can help. And sometimes I make decisions about Mom without consulting them, but it is too much effort to pick up the phone every time and ask their opinion.*
>
> *In truth, I'm not sure how they can help. What I really want is for them to share with the innumerable aspects of caring for Mom, but they can't do that. I know what I don't want — Judy's advice. Her telephone calls are real downers, not a word of appreciation. At least Tom doesn't make me feel worse. In fact, over the years he's become a much better listener. Perhaps that's what I want. I'd like my brother and sister to show an interest in how things are for me, to recognize that I'm doing well at a job that is not always easy. And I'd like them to visit when they can and give me a break.*

When you do visit, you may have difficulty taking your brothers' and sisters' concerns seriously. Your parents may seem to be doing well. What you may not realize is that your trips home are opportunities for a family celebration with your parents eager to put on a good show. Warned that you would find your parents discouraged, fatigued, or confused, you find them as competent and cheerful as they have ever been. What you see with your own eyes carries more weight than your siblings' warning about your parents' struggles. One of my clients, who tried for months to explain to her brother that their parents were finding their house too much work, was frustrated when during his visit they were energetic and uncomplaining and completely denied any problems. She knew that after he left, both parents would be exhausted and return to ruminating about possible moves. While her brother acknowledged that he was probably not seeing the true situation, she knew that he also believed she was exaggerating the difficulties.

Conversely, if you have not seen your parents for some time, you may see signs of deterioration more clearly than your siblings who live nearby. A slow but steady loss of stamina or memory may not be so noticeable to those who see their parents frequently and almost unconsciously learn to compensate. To you, the change can be dramatic, obvious, and startling. You may be tempted to ask such questions as, "Why haven't you taken her to the doctor?" or "Why didn't you tell me he was this bad?" Not surprisingly, your brother or sister hears not your distress at your parent's deterioration but criticism of their handling of the situation. Feeling maligned, they are likely to respond with anger and defensiveness. Tension builds if the visiting sibling goes on to make suggestions that put more of a burden on the caregiver. "Can't you invite her over more often?" may seem an innocuous suggestion to one who does not carry the weight of daily responsibilities.

Living at a distance brings other problems as well. Removed from the details of caregiving, you may feel left out or guilty because your siblings are taking the major responsibility. Given the realities of time and distance, it is difficult to know how to be involved, useful, and helpful without feeling superfluous or appearing to interfere.

Whether you are near or far, you each have an important perspective. Those of you separated by many miles cannot be involved with your parents on a daily basis, but can often see things not evident to those close to the situation. Those nearby see the daily problems in all their complexity and can be a source of information otherwise unavailable to their distant siblings. With goodwill, you can learn from each other.

One of my clients provided an example of conflict between siblings and an honest attempt to resolve it. Ann came to see me primarily because she was angry with her sister. Melissa lived about three hours drive from the town where both Ann and their mother lived. Their mother lived in her own apartment, but she was no longer able to be independent. Both her body and mind had deteriorated to the point that she needed daily help to eat properly and take her medication. Ann was the one who provided that help. Melissa, from a more distant vantage point, failed to see how impaired their mother was. When she invited her mother for a visit, she expected her mother not only to remember the conversation but also make her own transport arrangements. When the plans went awry, she was angry with Ann because she did not help with plans she knew nothing about. Time and time again, minor crises occurred because Melissa refused to recognize that their mother's memory was now completely unreliable as a link between her and her sister.

It took a great deal of effort on the part of both sisters, but they eventually learned to work as a team. Ann realized that she had assumed that her sister would see their mother's decline for herself. Melissa did not realize that when her mother recounted events, her imagination made up for the large gaps in her memory. As Ann became more explicit about the real situation, Melissa in turn became more supportive. She proved to be a good listener, and that was often all that Ann wanted. Now Melissa's visits were planned to give Ann some much needed relief. Their mother was always pleased to see Melissa, and Ann could see why. She breezed into the house with an energy that Ann felt she had lost forever. In her low moods Ann still resented her sister's carefree manner but she was able to appreciate the shedding of responsibility, if only for a short while.

It took longer for Ann to admit that Melissa's occasional differences of opinion sometimes had value. It was Melissa who saw that Ann could not continue to spend many hours each day with her mother and insisted that it was time to employ some help. For Ann, the burden of trying to find help seemed more than she could take on. She was grateful when Melissa said that she would do that. Now it felt as if the two of them were working together instead of against each other.

The Caregiver

If you are the caregiver, you know that providing practical and regular help is both a burden and a satisfaction. Most of the time you may feel that the negatives outweigh the positives. But you do have the satisfaction, denied to your more distant siblings, of doing something useful for your parents. This may create a new bond, or enhance an already existing one, between you.

The stress associated with caregiving may be minimal or considerable but is always significant, coming as it does atop your other responsibilities. It is especially heavy if you feel your effort is not recognized or appreciated by other members of the family. Study after study shows that the burden of caregiving is related in large part to the support the caregiver receives. Care is less of a stress when you are not left to do it alone and can expect support from others. Being part of a network of people who are concerned and helpful, even if you do most of the work, feels very different from doing the same amount of work alone.

After Mom came to live with us, I was busier than I thought possible. There was an overwhelming amount of work. In fact, time at my paid job was the most relaxed part of the day. The change was hard on my husband too. He didn't complain, but home was different. I was too tired to be any fun. I couldn't even stay awake by the time I sat down in the evenings. At first, we both looked forward to the weekends when Mom went to stay with Judy. But Mom usually returned from these visits so anxious that for a few days she tried not to let me out of her sight, following me from room to room. And at night she didn't sleep well. Frankly, the free weekend wasn't worth the upset. Then I found out that Judy sometimes left Mom with a "baby-sitter." I was shocked that Mom was left in an unfamiliar house with an unfamiliar person, and I guess my voice showed it. Judy snapped that I spoiled and overprotected Mom — "if you do everything for her she'll never do it for herself." But I know Mom and still think I'm right. So I started to make excuses for Mom not to visit, and I don't think Judy minded at all.

Most of the time I felt on an emotional roller coaster. I used to be pretty even tempered, but I lost it. I cried when the smallest thing went wrong, or I'd snap at the kids for no reason. But Tom and Judy are the two I should have been mad with. They had no appreciation of how our lives had changed and, as far as I can tell, didn't even want to know. Why should I have had to tell them how we're doing? If they were interested they would have asked. Besides, I didn't want to be always complaining.

But there is another side to taking care of Mom. On my good days, I feel pretty good about what we're doing. I'm proud of the way my kids and husband help out. Mom is a sweet person, which is a real blessing; she never complains and is so appreciative. I'm not sure that I want Tom and Judy to be more involved. We may be better off as we are.

If you are the main caregiver, you have to decide how much you will tell your siblings, whether to include them in all decisions, and exactly if, and how, they can help. If, like Pat, you expect them to be critical, uninterested, or generous with ill-considered advice you will be tempted to share little with them. On the other hand, if you can understand that their behavior originates in their feelings of useless-ness or rivalry, you may be able to reach out to them, and they may respond in a way that brings benefits to you all.

However hard you try to be honest about your own and your parents' situation, you may have siblings who continue to be un-interested or negative. At such times, it is tempting to cut them out completely. It takes too much effort to keep them involved. There may be another reason for not including your siblings. Feeling like the most important child to your parents can be so gratifying that you may be unwilling to share them. It is important to ask yourself whether you are being self-serving and contributing to the distance between members of your family.

Ignoring your siblings may work for a while as it reduces your irritation, but it will almost certainly create problems in the future. At some point they are likely to accuse you of keeping them in the dark, failing to consult them, and even making it difficult for them to be close to their parents. You are also denying your parents and yourself the possibility of help from them. By being open and willing to share, you do everything in your power to enable all of you to work together.

Only Children

Those of you with no brothers or sisters face a very different situation. You avoid many of the problems of negotiating, of com-municating, or of rivalry, but you do not have anyone with whom to share the responsibility as your parents become frail or needy. Though less emotionally complex than dealing with a number of family members, yours can be a lonely position. However patient your spouse or friends, there is no one you can count on to be as interested in your worries and thoughts about your parents as you are. If you had siblings, you would expect them to share your concerns, but, as it is, you may find yourself apologizing for boring or burdening others when you are preoccupied with your parents.

Relationships between only children and their parents are often intense. I remember one of my friends in college describing her feel-ings of guilty dread when she visited her parents because they were so consumed by the minutiae of her activities that she felt her life had become theirs. She wished she had siblings to dilute her parents' kindly but intrusive interest. This relationship between only children and their parents often becomes more intense when parents become frail or one parent dies. If your parents are dependent, their needs carry an extra weight because you are the only one to help. Widowed parents will often move to be near their children, further tightening a bond that was already emotionally close.

However difficult it may be to agree on how to help their parents, siblings do have a wider range of possibilities available to them. They offer differing skills and can coordinate visiting schedules and share chores. They can also support each other. Only children have fewer options. It is impossible to find anyone who understands what it is to be a child of these parents, to share the pleasures and the griefs, the problems and the decisions.

Spouses of only children tend to be more drawn into the care of their in-laws than those who have married into a large family. If you are an only child with some responsibility for your parent, your spouse's response to your involvement makes a considerable difference to you. It is the difference between feeling support and being caught by two conflicting loyalties. In your turn, it is important that you are sensitive to your spouse's feelings, that when choices have to be made, your parent does not automatically have priority over other members of your extended family.

Spouses of Adult Children

The family is a complicated organization, within which each member has a unique web of loyalties, influences, and responsibilities. One relationship that cannot be ignored is that of the in-laws. They can have either a moderating or exaggerating effect on interactions within the family. Their degree of involvement varies tremendously, from bystander to caregiver, from critic to empathic supporter. If their spouses are concerned with their parents, to a greater or lesser extent they will be involved too.

Soon after two people decide to live together, they have to make some decisions about how to relate to each other's parents. The issue surfaces dramatically at holidays as couples try to work out acceptable arrangements, sometimes spending hours on the road in their efforts to be fair to their families and each other. When parents age and grow frail, couples have to make more difficult decisions. Different values and levels of attachment have the potential to cause a rift between partners. A daughter may hold the view that children should care for their parents if that becomes necessary, whereas her husband may believe that all their time and energy should be put into their own immediate family. A daughter may find it difficult to spend time with her parents whom she remembers as critical and unloving, but her husband finds them enjoyable company and may not understand her intolerance.

Close bonds between parents and adult children can cause as much difficulty as distant or difficult ones. Spouses may feel neglected if their partners are closely connected with their parents: "When your mother calls, you're right there." "You do more for your parents than you do for me."

Many couples work together to meet their parents' needs, adding them to the responsibilities that they deal with as partners. This is an ideal collaboration. Other couples act like adversaries, resenting the time each spends with parents — time seen as depriving the rest of the family. In these circumstances, the caregiving child feels caught in the middle between needs of parent and spouse and unable to satisfy either.

Sometimes in-laws become more involved with a parent than the biological children. Daughters-in-law may become the significant caregivers, more knowledgeable and emotionally close than some of the natural children. Where there are no daughters, a family usually looks to the spouses of the sons to provide care. For the wife who has a job and responsibilities of her own this might feel like an unreasonable expectation.

However much they are involved with their spouse's parents, in-laws rarely have a full vote in any formal family discussion. They often feel they have responsibility but no authority. Family discussions can take on a political nature with agendas, often less than overt, as to who should attend, who should speak, and who should be counted. In-laws are rarely considered to be as important as natural children. In the absence of such consideration, they are likely to feel used and unappreciated, especially if they are involved in caregiving. If their contribution is recognized rather than taken for granted, they become a vital part of the caregiving team.

Whatever the formal process, spouses inevitably influence each other. Occasionally, an in-law may become a scapegoat as the rest of the family senses that this indirect influence is powerful and undermining their wishes. On the other hand, an in-law can be a more objective voice, providing a helpful perspective, because he or she does not have the lifelong personal history and feelings that come attached to that. Many people notice that they handle other people's parents more easily than their own, having more patience and tolerance with their parents-in-law than their spouse does. Their contribution is invaluable.

Stepparents

With the addition of stepparents and stepbrothers and stepsisters to the family picture, relationships become even more complicated. In our society, traditional nuclear families are becoming less common as divorces and remarriages occur, losing some members, adding others to the original group.

As adult children, most of you have strong feelings when your parents consider remarriage. You may be pleased that your parent has a companion for old age and be relieved at the lessening of responsibility for yourself. On the other hand, you may regard the prospect with dismay, feeling your parent is settling for too little. You may even consider that remarriage is in some way a betrayal of your dead parent, especially if the death was recent. A concern for some is that your inheritance will disappear, absorbed by a person your dead parent did not even know. If you and your parent had a close relationship, remarriage can feel like an unwelcome intrusion. You may have genuine concerns that the prospective mate is not a good one for your parent. Undoubtedly some suitors are motivated less by affection than by the promise of financial security or someone to look after them. There may be real danger that a parent will be taken advantage of.

Your concerns may be well founded but are more often based on your own feelings than on your parent's. You may not fully appreciate that elderly people who find themselves alone for the first time in their lives often feel very lonely, frightened, and even useless. For them, settling for a compatible companion may be more attractive than seeking an ideal soul-mate whose background and interests are the perfect match.

When you can identify the reasons for your doubts or dislike, you have a better chance of addressing them constructively. Far better to talk openly about any misgivings than to let them simmer. If you doubt the honesty of your parent's prospective partner, mention your misgivings — tactfully — or find a respected friend or professional acquaintance who would be prepared to do so. If your worry is about your relationship with your parent — that you will be less close after his or her remarriage — talk to your parent and consider planning time together without your partners. Concerns about inheritance can be handled by a prenuptial agreement. Or the couple may choose to live together without marrying. The latter step often causes waves among the family who are used to young members living together unmarried but are shocked if elderly people chose to do so. Sex between old people is often embarrassing for people to contemplate, especially when it applies to their parents.

Remarriage can prove to be a happy occasion for your whole family. Your parent may have a new lease on life with a relationship that is satisfying and energizing. You do not need to like your stepparent to appreciate what they bring to your parent. For some of you, your appreciation becomes affection as you form a relationship that is important in its own right.

When stepparents need care both they and you as their stepchildren are in uncertain territory. Much depends on how long you have known each other and the quality of your relationship. Unless you lived together during your childhood, you are unlikely to feel the same filial obligation and affection that you feel for your birth parents. It is also natural to assume that your stepparent's own children will do what is necessary. Given the complexity of human relationships, however, you may be pulled in to help with situations for which you feel no personal responsibility but which you see affecting your own parent. Faced with the prospect of watching your parent struggle to provide care for which he or she has insufficient strength, you may feel you have no alternative but to become involved.

There are happy circumstances when some of you may care for your stepparents willingly. You may have grown genuinely fond of your stepparent or be grateful for his or her care of your parent. In such cases, you may feel that your care and concern has been earned, and so give it freely.

Grandchildren

Grandchildren and grandparents often enjoy a relaxed and pleasurable relationship. With little history of conflict over rules or discipline, they are more tolerant of each other. It is the generation between them that often holds higher expectations, adheres to rules more rigidly, and takes failures more personally. Parents and children are both acutely sensitive to each other's perceived shortcomings — whether a forgotten birthday, a flash of irritation, an episode of thoughtlessness. Such lapses are often greeted with a smile or a shrug when they occur between grandparents and grandchildren. With this easier relationship, grandchildren who are involved in the care of their frail grandparents usually experience less sense of burden than their parents.

How children react to the physical and mental frailty of their grandparents depends largely on their age. Young children frequently

appear delightfully unconcerned by forgetfulness, confusion, or disability. They are more curious than repelled by aids such as walkers
and catheters; more interested in trying a wheelchair than bothered
by its meaning. As children grow older, so grows their discomfort
with ill health and disability, and they often prefer to keep their
distance. For young teenagers, discomfort becomes embarrassment,
especially if their friends are around. They may resist bringing friends
home if their grandparent is confused or behaves inappropriately.
Approaching adulthood, they usually grow more understanding of
what their grandparents are feeling and are able to respond with
some sensitivity.

If you are a caregiver with young children, much of your concern
will be about the effects on those children. As you expend time and
energy on your parents, you inevitably have less for your children. Is
it fair to change their lives? If so, how much? You are in a dilemma,
caught between your parents' needs and those of your children, with
insufficient resources to meet both as well as you would like. Where
there is serious conflict, your first priority has to be your children.

Children need to have parents sensitive to their needs most of
the time, and they do have needs that only parents can meet. This
does not mean, however, that you cannot provide the care for your
parents as well. Your children do not need you to respond to every
requirement instantly and may have to settle for less than they were
used to before their grandparents became sick. But you can lessen
the impact by setting aside some time to give them special attention.
If you bring your parents into your home, you can ensure that your
children have somewhere to retreat to when they need privacy. You
can also help them — and yourself — by talking about the process of
aging and about your children's feelings as they see their older relatives grow frail. Like all of us, children are more understanding and
deal with the changes more gracefully if their questions and concerns
are taken seriously.

Your children can gain satisfaction and self-esteem from taking
some responsibility for helping a frail older person. In ideal circumstances, the help they give makes them feel good about themselves
and more aware of the needs of others. Children do better with tasks
that are specific, personal, and within their capabilities. Again, as
parents you need to be sensitive to your children's feelings. They may
be happy to help their frail grandparents move around the house but
avoid going out with them in public. They may be anxious about
being left in charge, afraid that their grandparent might fall sick
or die. It is also important that their contribution is appreciated by

their grandparent, parent, or both. Children who see only that they are expected to be quiet, give up use of a room, or deal with tired grouchy parents are likely to feel little but resentment toward their grandparents.

Under some unfortunate circumstances, you may need to protect your children from your parents. Some older people, especially if they have a dementing illness, can be verbally abusive and are unable to alter their behavior. Your children should not be exposed to frequent, unfair criticism. At a young age they cannot understand that their grandparent's behavior is caused by an illness. If your parents are abusive and not living with you, you may decide not to take your children with you when you visit. In extreme situations, if your parents are in your home and your young children exposed regularly to unpleasantness, the hard reality may be that your parents have to leave.

Growth and Change

The increasing frailty of your parents can be an opportunity for rekindling old affections within the family and even developing a new appreciation of each other.

The fact that your parents are no longer autonomous shakes up the old order. Out of this shakeup come new responsibilities and challenges that may produce stress and conflict but can also lead to growth and satisfaction. You may be surprised to learn that you have the patience to sit and listen to the oft-repeated recollections of your mother. These changes are not limited to you as an individual. The members of your family may appear in a new light. A sister may be more thoughtful than you judged possible. You may see the "bossiness" of your brother from a different angle as he negotiates the financial maze of your parents' affairs.

Many brothers and sisters have much more contact with each other as their parents need help and they are called on to cooperate and make joint decisions. While it is true that some relationships rupture under the stress, many families find themselves growing closer as they see more of each other and work together.

Who Gets What?

Money matters are often an invisible and troublesome undercurrent that everyone tries to avoid. Whether there is little or plenty, money and material goods become an emotionally loaded issue. While your parent is living, you and your siblings may hold differing opinions about how your parent's money should be managed, by whom, and how it should be spent on your parent's care.

One matter that had never come up in our discussions about Mom's care was money. Well, that changed when we had to think about a nursing home for her. To my surprise, Tom was the one to make that suggestion. He and his wife had cared for Mom one weekend and that opened his eyes. We came home to find him exhausted and convinced that Mom was too much for us; and my husband agreed. At first, I hated to think of Mom in a nursing home, but I knew they were right. Judy and her husband didn't agree though. They wanted to see Mom's assets preserved as far as possible and considered nursing home care an outrageous expense that was possible to avoid. But Tom had finally come off the fence, and he can be forceful when he's determined. Anyway, Judy was not prepared to care for Mom, so she had no alternative but to agree.

One decision we'll have to make soon is what to do about Mom's belongings. The few nice things she has she brought with her to my house. And they're still there. Judy asked about them the other day, hinting that she'd like Mom's bedroom set for her daughter. I don't see that her daughter has any right to anything of Mom's. She hasn't taken any interest in Mom for years. On the other hand, I certainly don't want a fight with Judy.

You will almost certainly face this issue when your parents die, if not before. In our society, material goods become symbolic of feelings — of appreciation, of respect, of love. Your mother's ring may or may not represent some monetary value, but its real importance lies in the sentiments it stands for — everyone knows that. Siblings are usually less motivated by materialism than by concerns about who deserves what, who is getting more or less, who is going to "win." Quarrels are born of tensions that have been in existence for many years. The task of dealing with possessions may test your relationship with your siblings, stirring feelings of loss, competition, and jealousy.

There are fewer disagreements and hard feelings if you can all be clear about what you want and why. An object may be cherished for its special associations and sentimental value or for its financial worth. Before meeting to divide their parents' possessions, some siblings are able to work out a system which they agree is as fair as possible. They may decide to make individual lists of their ten most wanted items and hope there is not too much overlap. They may gather in their parent's old home, taking turns to select an item. Others may put their emphasis on monetary value and distribute possessions on that basis. In an attempt to avoid a potentially divisive task some children plan ahead, encouraging their parents to allocate their belongings while they are alive.

However you have to deal with your parent's affairs, it is important to allow sufficient time for the task. In the hope of settling matters as quickly as possible, some families distribute possessions without considering everyone's opinions, or impulsively decide on a sale, only to regret their decision later. Recognize that you need time to grieve and to appreciate the changes that have occurred. If your parent has just died, try to postpone dealing with your parent's house and belongings for a few weeks, even if it means making an additional trip.

You and your siblings will have a different experience emotionally. You each have your own level of attachment to your parents and to their home. Going through parents' belongings and papers, deciding what to throw away, what to keep, and what to give away can be both tedious and upsetting. Despite the difficulties, it will probably be a less distressing experience if you can do it with your siblings, but it may even be an important ritual of closure as you reminisce about your parents' lives.

Points to Consider

1. Develop a pattern of talking directly to your siblings rather than through your parent. It is impossible to have the working relationship you will need to develop without clear channels of communication.

2. Think about future problems. Discuss expectations and possible plans before the need arises. Include your parents if it is still possible.

3. When difficulties occur, share them with your siblings. Do not stop at venting, but also listen and be open to solutions other than your own.

4. Do not act alone if you can avoid it. Major decisions are best made jointly with everyone participating.

5. If you are the primary contact, keep the others informed. If they appear uninterested, continue to let them know what is

happening. Letters may work better than telephone calls. Such persistence may at best create a positive link with an estranged sibling, and at least prevent unjust accusations at a later date.

6. Be as honest as you can about your motives behind your suggestions and actions. Are you trying to exclude your sibling? Wanting to be your parent's favorite?

7. Ask your siblings for help. Be specific. They may not know what to offer. Then accept that they will do things in their own way. You cannot control everything.

8. If you are the distant one, ask your caregiving sibling how you can help. Make specific suggestions, rather than stopping at a vague "Let me know if I can do anything to help."

9. Try to appreciate the others' situations and feelings and recognize what they are doing for your parent.

10. If you are spending time, effort, and energy on your parents, remember that your spouse and children are affected too.

11. When it is time to dispose of your parents' possessions, be sensitive to each other's feelings. Try to take the time that you all need rather than impulsively making decisions you may regret later.

12. If you have to sort out your parents' belongings, consider doing it with your siblings. It may be the difference between a lonely, upsetting task and an important ritual that brings you and your siblings closer.

· *Chapter 7* ·

Coping with Physical and Mental Problems

❧

A NY TALK ABOUT AGING soon bumps into the subject of health. Are your parents still healthy, or are they beginning to have problems? Built into the question is the expectation that your parents' health will deteriorate as they age and that the subject concerns you as well as them. So much depends on the state of their bodies and minds — their sense of well-being, comfort, and, importantly for you, their need for help.

Health problems do increase greatly as people age. Two-thirds of the people over the age of sixty-five have at least two physical conditions for which they see their doctor. Two-thirds of all medications are prescribed to the oldest third of the population. When asked to determine which factors affect their satisfaction with their lives, most people put health at the top of the list. Interestingly, the important thing is how they perceive their health, not how it would objectively be assessed by an observer. Comparing themselves with others of a similar age, your parents may see themselves as in reasonably good shape and be content. They may judge their health as less of a problem than you do. They are interested primarily in whether they can do what they want to do and whether their independence is threatened.

You and your parents may disagree on how actively they should seek medical help. They may be reluctant, saying that their symptoms are "only to be expected," whereas you may see the need for professional attention. Or, in contrast, your parents may be preoccupied by their health, seeking help for conditions you consider minor. Physical problems arouse different emotions and carry different meanings for all of us. Illness is frightening. If your parents suspect that something is seriously amiss, ignorance may seem easier

129

to tolerate than knowledge. Or they may have had little experience with doctors and hospitals and prefer their pain or discomfort to what they do not know. Embarrassment is another powerful barrier. Many elderly men hesitate to talk to a physician about their sexual difficulties. For many elderly women, incontinence is such a painful secret that they stay indoors rather than seek help for a condition that is more common and treatable than they realize.

Physical problems in the elderly are often difficult to diagnose because they may show themselves in a different way than in younger people. For instance, an infection of the lungs or urinary tract may appear as confusion or apathy rather than as pain. If your parent has dementia and is unable to communicate about symptoms, diagnosis is a considerable challenge. As with young children, changes in the patient's behavior become the important signs that something is physically wrong. A client of mine noticed that her mother was eating poorly and seemed more reluctant than usual to get out of her wheelchair for a short walk. The staff of the nursing home agreed that she was more irritable when they had to move her, but otherwise she did not seem markedly different. A routine medical check revealed nothing. Knowing that her mother could not talk about how she felt, the daughter observed her particularly closely. She became certain that her mother was in pain, probably from her arthritis. After the doctor prescribed a regular pain medication, her mother quickly regained her appetite and normal easy-going personality.

Most physical problems can be treated. The treatment is often only partial, however. Unfortunately, older bodies do not work as well as young ones; aches and pains can be alleviated, disabilities adapted to, and symptoms lessened — but often not cured. Your parents probably have to live with some limitations, physically and possibly mentally.

Some conditions deserve special attention here because they particularly affect you also, and how you handle them will help or hinder your parents.

Hypochondriasis and Complaining

Many older people minimize physical changes and discomfort, but not all. There are people of all ages who are preoccupied with their health, who have low tolerance for pain and become upset by every sign and symptom they experience. Their doctors can assure them that they have no disease, but that is no comfort. They monitor their bodies constantly and limit their activities more than appears necessary. The aches and creaks of advancing years only increase their distress. Physical changes are not taken as inevitable nuisances to be adjusted to, but are viewed as fearful warnings of impending pain, disability, or even death.

If your parents' interests, activities, and even conversations are dominated by their bodily ills, you probably feel sometimes sad, often frustrated, and, all too frequently, bored. Tempting though it is to dismiss their pains as imaginary or exaggerated, your parents' pain is real. Pain does not have only physical causes. There are many other possible origins. It is frequently associated with depression and disappears if the depression is treated. It may come from fear of serious illness and death. For those who are watchful, even a healthy older body sends signals that can appear sinister. Any signs of sickness are frightening indeed. Occasionally, people so identify with a sick or dead loved one that they feel similar symptoms. And, in this culture, sickness can be an acceptable way of avoiding problems or unwelcome tasks and, above all, an effective means of seeking attention from doctors, nurses, and family. Whatever the reason for your parents' overconcern, lecturing or reasoning offer no reassurance. There is real pain of some sort. If you can recognize that, you may be able to help them tolerate the pain, or even eliminate it.

Another of my clients was disappointed that her mother refused to attend her granddaughter's wedding. It involved staying away from home for two nights. Her mother had occasional angina, though it had never been severe enough for her to take the nitroglycerine that she carried at all times. Her father, brother, and sister had all died of heart attacks. Her fear of being far from her doctor and the hospital was stronger than her wish to see her granddaughter married. When my client realized this, she and her mother were able to work around her fear. With her own doctor's reassurance that she could make the trip, with the name of a doctor and hospital at her destination should she need them, and the promise that any care would be coordinated with her own doctor, she was able to enjoy the wedding.

Illness and discomfort become even more compelling subjects of conversation if your parents have little else to occupy or distract them. They have plenty of time to think and worry about their health, which then becomes the main topic when you visit. They need to air their concerns to someone who cares, especially if they live alone or have no one else to confide in, but there may come a point when more talk does not ease their worry but rather perpetuates it. Then, gently turn the conversation to other matters.

Hearing

Hearing loss is widespread in the elderly. Although partially compensated for by a simple aid, it is a problem that is often misunderstood and has wide repercussions.

Loss of hearing may come on so slowly that both you and your parents may mistake it for other conditions. They notice that people are not speaking clearly, failing to tell them what is going on, or even deliberately excluding them from conversations. You notice that your parents show less interest in participating in general conversations, sometimes take notice and sometimes not, and frequently respond inappropriately to what others say. If you have tried to understand a language in which you are not fluent, you know how quickly you become exhausted from the effort. Similarly, your parents' apparent exhaustion, lack of interest, or confusion may be the result of poor hearing rather than contrariness, depression, or brain deterioration.

Hearing aids, even when they work well, are poor substitutes for good hearing. Difficult to get used to, they require so much patience and persistence that your parents often grow discouraged and give up the effort. Aids are particularly troublesome in large social gatherings, as they pick up a confusing array of sounds that normal ears screen out. Consequently, your parents may avoid occasions where there are more than one or two people, and so become isolated in their own world.

As deafness can contribute to isolation, so can isolation contribute to paranoia and distorted thinking. If your parents rarely talk to other people and are cut off from television, radio, and telephone, they may come to regard the world as a suspicious place, populated by people who intend harm.

Alcohol Abuse

Although the abuse of alcohol among the elderly creates fewer social problems than in younger age groups, it is a serious issue in many families. And with the elderly alcoholism is often a secret — hidden, unrecognized, and rarely addressed.

Alcoholics in old age fall into two groups: those who have abused alcohol all their lives, and those who started to drink heavily for the first time when they became old.

Denial is a notorious feature of alcoholism. If your parents have been drinking consistently and heavily for many years, they have probably always denied that alcohol has any ill effects on them or their behavior. As they reach old age, you may notice that they are affected by smaller amounts of alcohol than in the past. Heavy use of alcohol over a long period has serious effects on the body. Add these assaults to the general wear and tear of a long life and, just as with medication, older bodies become more sensitive to alcohol and react more dramatically than when they were young.

There are other reasons why even small amounts of alcohol cause problems for some older people. Many medications and illnesses do not mix well with alcohol, producing more symptoms and side effects than either would alone. If your parents have Alzheimer's disease, you may notice that they are more confused and irritable after even one drink.

A woman came to see me about her mother who had lived alone for many years but recently was not doing well. On two occasions her daughter had noticed bad bruises on her mother's arm and face. Her mother reported vaguely that she had fallen. She had been a heavy weekend drinker for much of her adult life and had increased her intake considerably after she retired from work. As her mother became physically frail, her daughter took over the shopping and with it the control of alcohol entering the house. She did buy one bottle of wine a week, hoping that this would appease her mother and do no harm. She was in her mother's home often enough to know that the wine was not drunk all at one time. What was happening, however, was that her mother's ability to tolerate alcohol was so diminished that a fraction of her once-habitual intake had a serious effect on her balance.

Some people start to drink heavily in old age because they are bored, depressed, or in pain. One of the hazards of retirement is the opportunity to drink during the day. Gone is the routine of the working week that for many imposed limits on alcohol intake. Loneliness is also commonly at the root of alcohol abuse. In the same vein, people who have problems with their memory may inadvertently up their intake, believing that each drink is their first.

If you are concerned about your parents' drinking, it is probably difficult to talk to them about it. You can only give your opinion with as much love as possible, and encourage others to do the same. Ultimately, however, your parents will and must make their own decisions to drink or not, just as they decide whether to smoke, eat junk food, or exercise.

Though you have little power to control their drinking, you do have the right to control how your parents' behavior affects you. If you do express your concern and your parents persist in drinking too much, you will need to find ways to avoid contact with them if the situation becomes unpleasant. The principles of detachment taught by such groups as Al-Anon have helpful applications for anyone dealing with alcohol abuse in others, even if full-blown alcoholism is not the issue.

For those with a less serious problem, confrontations will sometimes work. If you make it clear that your reluctance to visit is related to your parent's drinking, it may have an ameliorating effect. An elderly client of mine admitted that his two evening drinks had increased to four since his wife had become sick. The alcohol helped him relax, although he did complain of poor sleep and being "fuzzy" in the morning. Two weeks after I expressed concern about his drinking, he visited his physician who voiced the same concern. He was so impressed that two people he respected were united in their opinion and cared enough to say so that he cut back to one drink and maintained that with little difficulty.

It is never too late to stop abusing alcohol. Many older people respond well to treatment. One of my clients surprised himself and his family by successfully completing a treatment program at the age of seventy-nine years. Not only did he feel a personal sense of accomplishment, but he had new friends and a support group largely made up of younger men. Above all, his children and grandchildren were finally pleased to spend time with him.

For those who are addicted, treatment usually has to start in an in-patient unit with "detoxification" and therapy that then continues on an out-patient basis. Alcoholics Anonymous is a powerful support group that helps countless people combat the disease and maintain sobriety.

Medication

Medication is clearly an essential component of health care, and most people need it at many times in their lives, especially as they age. There can be harmful side effects, however. Just as bodies experience sickness and alcohol differently as they age, so do they respond differently to medications. A small dose of a mild sedative may induce extreme lethargy or poor balance, both potentially dangerous in a frail person. Of all the parts of the body, the brain appears the most susceptible to medication or any substance that comes from the outside. Anaesthesia, for instance, is frequently experienced by the older brain as an assault, to which it may react with gross confusion and hallucinations that take a day or two to clear.

Elderly bodies are not only more sensitive to the effects of medication, but they also store the substance for a longer period. The kidneys are less efficient as cleaning agents. Consequently, doses usually need to be lower for the elderly than for younger people.

Despite these hazards, the average elderly person needs to take several different medications. Put together several different medications, different doses at various times of day, failing eyesight, and a little forgetfulness, and the result can be a problem. For good measure add several doctors prescribing medications that possibly diminish or enhance the effects of each other, and the problem is serious.

Medication bought over the counter may be particularly open to misuse or even abuse. Many people assume that because it is readily available it is not harmful and can be used freely. "If one is helpful, three will be more so" is a dangerous assumption made by many.

If your parents develop new signs of confusion, apathy, nervousness, or agitation it is quite possible that improper medication, or improper use, is the cause. It is important to check that they are taking correctly what has been prescribed and that they are using nonprescription drugs appropriately. Seek medical advice if necessary. Doctors or even pharmacists can probably tell you about the compatibility of medicines.

Hospitalization

A hospital is not a comfortable place for any of us to be. Hospital routines are especially ill suited to older people. Strange surroundings, frightening and painful procedures, harsh noises, and many unfamiliar people can create a nightmarish set of circumstances for an older person — particularly if any degree of dementia is involved. If your parents were frail before they were admitted, hospitals often have a negative effect mentally and emotionally.

Like all hospital patients, your parents have to give up a great deal of control. They are exposed to all kinds of intrusions. They are fed, bathed, and told what to do until some feel as if their bodies no longer belong to them. They will react in their own ways. "Good" patients submit passively, not protesting or asking too many questions, whereas "bad" patients rebel, refuse to follow advice and question everything. If your parents are compliant, they will have an easier hospital stay and are certainly more pleasant for the staff, but if they become dependent, looking for others to do everything for them, they emerge from the hospital less willing and less able to care for themselves. There is some evidence that patients who strive to retain more autonomy than the hospital readily allows actually recover more quickly from illness and surgery. It is a difficult line to tread, however, because assertiveness that becomes aggression and questions that become demands can drive staff and necessary care away.

The challenge is to maintain as much control as is compatible with the realities of the situation. In the hospital, much has to be taken on trust by patients if the medical staff are to have the time and opportunity to do their jobs. But there are good reasons why people should ask questions about the course of their illness, learn what to expect from procedures, and be given information about alternative treatments or nontreatment.

Your parents may need you as an advocate. If they are sick enough to be in the hospital, their capacities to think clearly or understand what is happening to them are probably limited. You can encourage them to be active participants in their care, but you may have to be the spokesman, translator, information seeker, and buffer.

Forgetfulness and Confusion

If the thought of physical illness is frightening, the prospect of brain disease is terrifying. "As long as I don't lose my mind" reflects the greatest fear of most us as we contemplate old age, both for ourselves and those we love. That we might lose our ability to think, to recognize others, to be ourselves, fills us with horror. Unfortunately, our brains do deteriorate, sometimes temporarily, sometimes permanently.

As they age, brains, like bodies, become more sensitive to change and susceptible to damage. If your parents become confused, it may be the first sign that they are physically or emotionally sick. Pneumonia, for instance, may first reveal itself, not as difficult breathing but as unusual vagueness and forgetfulness. The effects of anaesthesia, hospitalization, and grief may all look like brain disease. For the most part, these symptoms are temporary and will clear as your parents recover from the primary illness or upset.

There are, of course, some diseases that cause severe and permanent memory loss and confusion. When they occur, these conditions are some of the great tragedies of old age. While they are not the sole province of the elderly — they can and do attack young people — dementing illnesses are more likely to develop in old age. It is not true, however, that people inevitably "lose their minds" if they live long enough.

Even normal brains work differently as they grow older. One change is that they slow down somewhat. Healthy older people seem to perform as accurately on intelligence tests as younger people, but they need more time to complete the job. For most of us, learning new tasks takes longer the older we become, but when it comes to performance, experience can often compensate for lack of speed.

Another change, and one that is annoying to most people, is that memory becomes less efficient. When I give a talk about Alzheimer's disease and mention memory loss as the first sign, there is almost always an audible shifting of chairs in the audience. Most of us over the age of fifty notice that we do not remember as well as we used to. There is such a thing as benign memory loss of old age — "benign" because it is not the result of disease. It is a problem of recall. The information is there, in our head, we know it is there but it is temporarily out of reach. These minor memory lapses are irritating and sometimes embarrassing but usually *not* a sign that brain pathology or dementia is developing.

Senile dementia or severe deterioration of the elderly brain is the result of injury from trauma or disease, not of old age. The two most common forms of senile dementia are Alzheimer's disease and multi-infarct dementia. Multi-infarct dementia is caused by a large number of tiny strokes, each damaging a small part of the brain.

Alzheimer's disease has received a great deal of attention in the past fifteen years, but it is not a new illness — it was first described in 1907 by German physician Alois Alzheimer. Because it is more common in old age and more people are living to be old, it is more widespread now than in the past. A large percentage of nursing home residents have the disease and, with life expectancy continuing to increase, it is a social and personal problem that will grow larger as the baby boom generation reaches old age.

Alzheimer's disease is not easy to diagnose. The only definitive test is a microscopic examination of brain tissue which, for obvious reasons, cannot be done until after death. For practical purposes, it is a diagnosis by exclusion. Other diseases have to be considered and eliminated, leaving Alzheimer's disease as the probable answer. In addition to short-term memory loss, other early symptoms are decline in ability to use judgment, intelligence, and reason. As the disease progresses to its later stages, its victims lose most of their memory, including the ability to follow a conversation and recognize their family; they are confused most of the time, and become unable to care for their basic needs. It is rare that someone can be cared for at home throughout the course of the disease. It lasts a long while, usually eight or more years, from the time of diagnosis to death, and by the end, most patients need professional, twenty-four-hour care that can be provided only in a nursing home.

Personality changes vary greatly from patient to patient. Some people remain sweet and easy to please whereas others have mood swings, erupting into extreme agitation or suspiciousness. While such changes in character are ravaging, there will be glimpses of the "pre-Alzheimer's personality" even in the advanced stages of the disease. One of the interesting things I have noted through years of Alzheimer support groups is that the disease tends to exaggerate the personality traits that were present through much of the victims' lives. If a parent has always been gentle and sociable, he or she will probably continue to respond positively to people and generally be agreeable. If a parent has always liked to be in control, he or she may become very difficult to please, fiercely refusing help with anything. The disease erodes the layers of social behavior that taught us to moderate anger, delay our wishes, and cover up our impatience. As these layers wither away, people suffering from Alzheimer's disease may loudly protest their dislike of visitors, be unable to wait for food to be served, and become irritable at any frustration.

Dementia of all kinds is a heartbreak for the family of the victims as much as the victims themselves. Perhaps more so.

If your parents have Alzheimer's disease, your life is profoundly affected too. As your parents become less able, you and your family have to take over more and more of their responsibilities. The problem is that in the early stages your attempts at help are frequently rebuffed. *You* notice that they forget appointments, pay bills twice or not at all, or lose their possessions, but they are rarely aware of their decline. You are in the frustrating position of taking over tasks that you do not want — driving, paying bills, doling out medication — and that your parents probably do not want to relinquish. Your persuasion and reason do not often work. You try to explain why they cannot have the car keys or leave the house alone, and they may agree with you. Within a short while, however, they act as if your conversation never took place, which of course, for them, it has not. Again and again, you have to deal with the same question as if they were asking it for the first time.

Some tasks are particularly difficult for your parents to give up. Driving a car and handling money are aspects of being an independent person. Most of us remember acquiring these symbols of adulthood, and hate the prospect of losing them. One of my clients had to take control of her mother's checkbook because her mother was buying expensive cosmetics and jewelry that she neither needed nor could afford. Initially, her mother agreed to the plan but later objected strenuously. As far as she could understand, she had controlled her money all her life and could continue to do so. It may be a real dilemma for you to provide care and safety in a way that does not further erode your parents' self-esteem. Unfortunately, this is not always possible, but if you are sensitive, thoughtful, respectful, and gentle you will be successful much of the time.

People react differently to the decline of their mental capacities. Some seem to be unaware of what is happening to them, suffering no anxiety or depression. Others are painfully conscious that there is something wrong with them. As the disease progresses, your parents' fear may become more primitive. Unable to make sense of their world, they cling to those they trust, following you from room to room, afraid to be left alone. You may hope that a trip will be a pleasant change of scene, but for your parents it is a nightmare of confusion. New situations are full of uncertainties. And for a person with no memory, every situation is new. Even daily routines can become problems. Just as very young children may be afraid of going down the drain with the bath water, your parents may be terrified at the prospect of getting into a tub. They cling for reassurance to the familiar, but fewer and fewer things are familiar.

If you spend a lot of time with your parents, you become the key to their comfort. You probably notice that they have an uncanny ability to reflect your mood. If you are irritable, they become anxious and edgy; if you can remain calm and good humored, so do they. As they lose their abilities, whether to find their belongings or to make themselves understood, your parents become frustrated and upset. If you respond in kind, they may become extremely agitated, and even aggressive. Extreme agitation coupled with violent behavior is sometimes called a catastrophic reaction. Difficult though it often is, if you are quiet and reassuring, your parents will calm down.

With the best intentions in the world, you cannot always remain peaceful and gentle. Do not punish yourself for this. Fatigue and short temper are part of being human, and caring for a parent who has dementia tests the patience of anyone. Fortunately, the disease that robs its victims of their faculties also removes their ability to hold a grudge. Your parents will have forgotten your bad temper long before you have.

Care of a person with Alzheimer's disease is demanding and time-consuming but also emotionally wrenching. This disease robs its victims of their personhood. As one of my clients said, "I'm caring for my mother's body, but the woman I grew up with and loved no longer exists." You desperately want your parents to be the way they were. Describing a visit to his mother in the hospital, Russell Baker wrote, "For a time I could not accept the inevitable. As I sat by her bed, my impulse was to argue her back to reality." It is a feeling shared by everyone in that position. So you may try to will your parents to remember your name, recognize your children, get better. But disease has reduced your parents' world to its essentials. Names, dates, information become irrelevant. The same client told me that she found it useful to ask herself the question "Does it matter if it is Tuesday?" This helped her realize that many things are not ultimately very important. It slowly became easier for her to accept her mother as she was at that moment and to let go of what had been. What matters to your parents is that they feel secure, comfortable, and loved.

At present no one knows the cause of Alzheimer's disease and there is no treatment, except to relieve some of the symptoms. Agitation, sleeplessness, and depression usually respond to medication. The most effective treatment continues to come from the people who provide care. If your parents feel safe, have a set routine, live in a calm atmosphere where too much is not expected of them, they are usually comfortable.

Suspiciousness

Occasionally, people become suspicious as they age, and if this happens, they are likely to be suspicious of those close to them. You may become the target, blamed and mistrusted by your parent for no apparent reason.

Suspiciousness can be a result of several physical or mental conditions. If your parents are deaf, it is easy for them to think that people are talking about them when they are out of earshot. At a more severe level, even to the point of paranoia, suspicion is more often a symptom of brain disease, particularly Alzheimer's disease. Troubling though it is to deal with, it does have a certain logic and does serve a purpose. When things go wrong, most people try to save face, and blaming others is a way — albeit a clumsy one — of doing that. It is less discomforting for your parents to think that you have stolen keys or money than to admit that they cannot remember where they put them, and, what is worse, that they have no chance of remembering. Their belief effectively saves them from recognizing their decline, and so preserves their self-esteem.

The delusion and blame are difficult to handle, however. There is no bridging the gap between your truth and theirs. Your usual resources of reason and common sense do not work. People with a dementia do not *decide* to blame someone else to avoid the embarrassing truth; they truly believe their explanation. If you contradict them, a fruitless argument will ensue, followed by frustration and spiraling tempers. You can probably restore calm if you accept what your parents are feeling, but avoid agreeing or disagreeing with their delusion. If you are accused of stealing your parents' car, for instance, and you can quietly agree that they must hate not having a car to drive, there is a good chance that they will become less agitated and able to be distracted into some other activity.

It is always painful to be blamed unjustly and to hear your parents describe you in unflattering terms — inattentive, uncaring — which you know are not true. Discomfort can become embarrassing if your parents complain to friends and neighbors that you are stealing their belongings or money. It is usually obvious to others, however, that your parents are confused and forgetful about many things, including the whereabouts of possessions. Few people will label you as a thief. They are more likely to be understanding and even helpful if you can explain to them what is wrong.

Remembering that there is a disease at work may help you not to take the accusations personally. Your confused parents are not thinking of you as an untrustworthy or unloving person, but often the only explanation that makes sense in their chaotic world is that someone is being deliberately unhelpful or mean. In all likelihood, once the incident has passed, they will forget their suspicions. Unfortunately for you, your memory is not so short. A sense of humor, where possible, eases the sting.

Depression

Given the changes that people have to face in old age, it is surprising that depression does not affect everyone. In fact, studies indicate that in the present generation of old people depression is less common than in younger age groups. The reason for this is not clear, because on the face of it the elderly have more to be depressed about. There are various conjectures. It is possible that those who do not become depressed are more likely to survive to old age. There is also evidence that the present group of old people have not suffered much from depression at *any* age. We may see a very different picture as new generations reach later life. Some experts, however, believe that depression among the elderly is underreported and often unrecognized, and so more widespread than statistics show. Whatever the general picture, it is certainly true that for many individuals depression is a significant and painful illness, and one that your parents may experience.

Depression comes in various guises, ranging from extreme listlessness to an agitated inability to sit still, from a pervasive feeling that life has no pleasure, to attempts at suicide. All of us periodically suffer from low moods that last several hours or days. They are uncomfortable but do not interfere with our usual activities. We still get out of bed in the morning, fix meals, do our work. The depression that is a mental illness bears some resemblance to these normal mood fluctuations, but is more disabling. People with a clinical depression, or melancholia, as it is sometimes called, find their mood dominated by a hopelessness and despair that they cannot shake. They often eat and sleep poorly, feel fatigued, and show little interest in anything outside themselves. The world becomes a very gray place indeed.

My first experience with serious depression came when a nurse called the clinic expressing concern about her seventy-seven-year-old neighbor who had become increasingly withdrawn over the past few weeks and was often in bed, apparently uninterested in eating or even talking. When I went to the house, there was no response to my knock. I opened the door and could just hear a faint "Come in" from the next room. I found Mrs. Wilson in the dark, slowly rocking in her chair. With obvious effort she raised her eyes momentarily to look at me, but then her head sunk back to its bowed position. The only sound was the slow creaking of her chair. Her apathy was extreme. Every activity seemed to require more energy than she had. She did not resist my offer of a cup of tea, but she only sipped it if I prompted her. Talking was painfully slow, long pauses separating the few words that took so much effort to produce.

Depression is not often as profound as it was for Mrs. Wilson. Even in its less severe forms, however, it is a painful condition that robs its sufferers of joy and vitality. Mrs. Wilson had had periodic depressions throughout her life, but for some people depression may come for the first time in old age. Loss of good health, chronic pain, change of house, retirement may all precipitate feelings that life is not worth living, and never will be again.

Another client, Mrs. Sanders, presented a more typical example of depression. She was brought to the clinic by her daughter. Her first complaint was that she felt unwell — her stomach hurt, her head felt fuzzy, and she was tired all the time. She had never felt like this before. "I am a stranger to myself," she said. I learned that Mrs. Sanders had just moved from her home in suburban Washington, D.C., where she had lived for fifty years, to Vermont so that she could be closer to her only child, Alice. Initially enthusiastic about the move, she soon became negative, complaining about everything. Her daughter could not believe the change in her. For years her mother had lived alone, done her own cooking, driven her car, and led a full and active social life. Now she did not want to meet people, showed little interest in making her apartment into a comfortable home, and seemed incapable of making decisions. She was on the phone several times a day, begging her daughter to visit and stay with her or take her to the doctor about some new pain. When the doctor could find nothing physically wrong, Alice hoped that time would help. Her mother had made a huge change and needed time to adjust. But the situation got worse. By the time I met them, Mrs. Sanders was listless and dispirited. She would occasionally wander around the house making half-hearted attempts to tidy up or get herself something to eat. When Alice visited, which she did at least daily, her mother would rally but would not want her to leave. Alice was growing increasingly desperate. Nothing she did helped.

Mrs. Sanders was evaluated by a doctor and began therapy. Within the next few weeks, she began to improve. As anti-depressant medication took effect, her mood lifted, her physical complaints disappeared, and she had more energy. In therapy sessions she faced the losses she had experienced and her anger and disappointment that Alice had not asked her to live with her. Sometimes Alice joined her for a session, and together they were able to examine their relationship and what they could realistically expect of each other. As Mrs. Sanders improved, she returned to the person she and her daughter both recognized — active, social, and self-sufficient.

As with other health problems in older people, depression is not always easy to identify. One of the reasons for underreporting is that depression often looks and feels like physical illness. Many old people do not consciously feel sad, but they do feel unwell. They are more likely to take their loss of appetite, fatigue, and vague aches and pains to their general physicians than to mental health workers. In turn, their physicians are more reluctant to refer them to a specialist than they would a younger patient.

Older people represent a small proportion of the patients at mental health clinics. Among the reasons usually cited are the stigma attached to mental illness and the acceptance of depression in the elderly as "to be expected" by physicians, families, and even the elderly themselves. The evidence, however, is that older people do well when they receive appropriate treatment.

Depression is an illness that can be treated. Most patients are treated as out-patients, though a hospital stay may sometimes be necessary, especially for those who feel suicidal. Many medications are useful in the treatment of depression, and counseling or psychotherapy can help a patient identify and deal with the feelings that precipitated or contributed to the illness. Medication and "talking therapy" can be used separately or together. Occasionally, electroconvulsive therapy is recommended. Despite its poor reputation, largely due to its overuse in the past, this treatment can produce dramatic and quick results for severely depressed patients and, because it has few side effects, is sometimes the chosen treatment for older people. (It worked exceedingly well for Mrs. Wilson, who, within two weeks of her first treatment, had so regained her friendliness and sense of humor that she was a favorite on the ward. Within another week she returned home.)

If your parents become depressed, your role is vital throughout their illness and recovery. Like all illnesses, depression affects not only the sufferers but those who care for or about them. You will probably find your parents' depression more difficult to understand than physical illness, and more trying. Because it affects the way your parents think and feel, this illness robs them, and you, of the tools you usually depend on to make things better. Bright conversation, distraction, suggestion, reason, all seem ineffective.

Your first task may be to recognize that your parents are suffering from a condition that needs professional help. Sudden personality changes, confusion, apathy, complaints of various and vague physical symptoms are no more normal in an older than a younger person. It is important for you to recognize that a sense of meaninglessness and despair are not anyone's fault. Therapy and medication are important components of the treatment of this illness but so are support, love, and patience, and these are the ingredients that you are best able to provide.

Loss of the Will to Live

What does it mean if your parents say that they no longer want to live? Is it a passing mood? Is it a cry for help? Is it a reasoned decision that they have come to after evaluating the quality of their life? It is always a painful thing to hear. It may even feel like a personal blow ("Surely I am enough reason for you to want to live") or a criticism ("If I did more or better she wouldn't feel that way"). It is always a sentiment to take seriously. Hard though it is to put your own feelings aside, try to listen carefully to your parents and understand what they are saying.

It is difficult for us to live a life that has lost its meaning. Elderly people are particularly vulnerable to this loss. Not only do they miss the activities and people whom they valued and loved — work, spouses, friends — but they no longer have as many requirements and expectations that were essential to their identity. Your parents in old age may have to struggle to feel that their lives have any relevance at all.

One of my older clients was wondering why she was feeling so dispirited after she had placed her husband in a nursing home. Looking back over her life she could see that she had coped with many changes and hardships much more easily than she was coping with this one. "Positive" and "flexible" were words she used to describe herself. She decided there was one huge difference between her current situation and the heartbreaks of her past. Her first husband died leaving her with small children to care for. Her daughter was killed at a time when her present husband was sick and dependent on her. Now, for the first time in her adult life she had no one except herself to care for. For her, looking after herself did not seem important enough. She was grieving not only the absence of her companion of many years but the work that had given a focus to her day. Difficult and trying though it had been to look after her failing husband, she could never doubt that she was essential. Suddenly her days were empty. Nothing seemed worth doing.

It is this sense of being unimportant to anyone that your parents may be articulating when they say that they do not want to live anymore. "I've been put out to pasture." "I've outlived my time." This is a cry for help. People get much of their feeling of well-being from relationships with others, and it is difficult to feel good if those contacts are only occasional and superficial. Protesting to your parents "Of course you are important to me" is unlikely to help them unless you back up your words with action. Spending time together, asking for support or advice, showing affection, letting your parents know you love them are all immensely important.

The feeling that life is not worth living, and furthermore that it never will be, is a common symptom of depression. People who are severely depressed may truly believe that those they love will be better off without them. For these people, suicide is a real risk. White elderly men have one of the highest suicide rates of any population group. Not all self-induced deaths are listed as suicide. Some people passively give up the will to stay alive. They stop eating, stay in bed, and throw away their medications. When this happens, psychiatric treatment is essential. As the illness lifts so does the sense of despair.

What about the people whose wish to end their life is not the despair of depression, but a considered opinion that life has too little quality to prolong? They may be dying, in pain, they may be so compromised physically that life holds no pleasure, they may be deeply weary of waiting for death. Sometimes they do take whatever steps they can to speed the process.

A woman in her mid-eighties came to see me because she was finding it difficult to adjust to all the changes in her life. She had been very active and fit until a few months earlier when she had had a heart attack. Her heart suffered enough damage that she was now leading the life of a semi-invalid. She was able to live alone, just. She could not bear to consider the future, "I hope I go fast before I have to give up my independence totally." Over the months she was able to make a somewhat satisfactory life for herself, but then she had another heart attack, which left her more debilitated, dependent on oxygen and a large array of medications. She began to talk about wanting to die. She had had a good life, but now pain and discomfort were dominating her days, leaving room for nothing else. Within a few weeks she was back in the hospital. She told me that she had decided to refuse all medications. She had talked to her daughter, who gave her blessing to her decision. The emotional cost of prolonging her life for a few more weeks or months had become too high.

Most people's hopelessness can be alleviated. There are many ways of trying to restore your parents' sense of meaning. Depression can be treated, physical pain controlled, grief shared and given time to heal, the wish to die understood. Your willingness to listen and understand will lessen the pain and the isolation that makes pain worse. Your unique contribution is to help provide your parents with a place in the world and a sense that they continue to be important, not necessarily for what they can do but for who they are and for as long as they live. But if they are ready to die before death is ready for them, stay close emotionally and ease their time of waiting as best you can.

Points to Consider

1. As your parents become frail, note any deterioration in their health and guide them toward appropriate assistance if they need help finding it.

2. Try to ensure that your parents have one physician who coordinates medical care, including medication.

3. If you suspect that your parents are not communicating well with the doctor or failing to remember instructions, ask them if you can talk or write to their doctor yourself. Most physicians welcome observations from concerned family members.

4. If your parents complain about their health more than appears justified by their condition, try to understand what is behind their distress. Is it fear of serious illness, need of attention, grief, depression, lack of activity, boredom?

5. Parents who need hearing aids will also need some understanding and encouragement while they become accustomed to them. Their sense of isolation can be severe.

6. If your parent is falling or seems more confused in the evenings, check whether alcohol or misuse of medications is the reason.

7. A pharmacist can be a useful ally in spotting inappropriate use of medications. Encourage your parents to use one pharmacist who keeps records.

8. If your parents forget to take medications as prescribed, there are special organizational boxes available at drugstores. Pills can then be set out a day or a week at a time.

9. While your parents are in the hospital, especially if they are very sick or confused, try to arrange for one family member to be well informed about their care, to communicate with staff, and to serve as an advocate as needed.

10. If your parents have a dementing illness, you will experience sadness and frustration over a condition that may persist for years. Your parents' moods will be much influenced by your level of patience and humor. When you are irritable or impatient, however, remember to understand that you too are human.

11. If your parents are confused, forgetful, or suspicious, let friends and neighbors know what is wrong. People are more likely to be helpful if they are not left to guess.

12. If your parents become suspicious and make accusations that have no basis in reality, their symptoms need medical attention. Try to keep calm and avoid argument.

13. Depression is a treatable illness. It should be taken as seriously in old people as in young.

14. Everyone needs to feel a purpose in life. Try to help your parents believe they have some value and a contribution to make.

· Chapter 8 ·

Letting Go
Without Turning Away

❧

A S YOU ADD ON WORK and responsibilities when caring for
your parents, you will also find there are some things you
have to let go. This may be the more painful task, demanding a clear head and rigorous self-honesty. Your image of yourself in
relation to your parents may be out of date or more influenced by
fantasy than reality. These are the images you have to let go. You
must have the courage to look unblinkingly at who you and your
parents are now. This is no time for false expectations. Unless your
attempts to help are based on the realities of your situation, they are
likely to misfire.

The first thing you may have to release is your picture of your
parents as they were. Old age changes them, sometimes a little, but
often a great deal. As they decline in physical and mental strength,
they will be less likely to meet your expectations than they ever were.
If you have unfulfilled expectations of respect and intimacy, you have
to let them go. Similarly, if you thought of your parents as paragons
of strength, it may no longer be reasonable or fair to expect them to
live up to your standards.

In caring for your parents, there are many obstacles between the
ideal and reality. You also have to adjust what you expect of yourself. All too often you find that your care falls short of what you
would like it to be. Time, resolve, money, energy are more limited
than you anticipated. You may often fail to be patient and loving.
You have commitments, live at a distance, have bad health, or find
your parents difficult. Your parents may be demanding, favor your
sibling, or be unappreciative and critical. Despite the limits imposed
by your situation and by the feelings you have for each other, you

149

probably choose to try to help in some way. Children who elect to do nothing are rare. The challenge is to let go of your unrealistic expectations and hopes while providing what you are able, to be responsible without putting yourself in a situation untenable for you.

As Parents Change

As your parents age, you have to give up the picture, formed when you were a child, that they are always strong, dependable, and in charge. By their eighth or ninth decade, even healthy parents need some special attention. They may not be able to take long trips alone. They may worry and lose sleep over problems they once took in their stride. And if your parents are not healthy, the changes can be dramatic. They may not be able to care for themselves, or even remember your name.

For decades, your parents were the most powerful people in your life, and, though their influence diminishes over time, you probably retain some vestige of your earlier belief that they would be there for you forever. They will be ready to protect, comfort, and help if necessary. You want them to see your children graduate and marry, to be interested in your success, to comfort you when you grieve. But with declining physical and mental health they may be unable, not only to care *for* you, but they may understand so little that they cannot even care *about* you. Their frailty rocks the ground you stand on. None of us is quite ready to give up on the reassurance our parents have provided. Small wonder that many of us try not to see our parents' decline, searching for signs that nothing is wrong, or that with time or appropriate treatment they will return to normal.

You will react to the decline of your parents in many ways. You will feel sad and worried, but, unexpectedly and guiltily, you will sometimes feel shame, distaste, and resentment. You may be particularly distressed by visible signs that your parents are not who they were. When your fashion-conscious mother begins to wear clothes that do not match and your fastidious father does not notice that he is drooling, you cannot deny their decline. One woman I know was forced to acknowledge the change in her father when he called her into the bedroom because he could not find the light switch. When she went in to help, she found him standing naked in the middle of the room. Surprised and embarrassed, she tried to avert her eyes, but her normally modest father seemed oblivious and made no attempt to cover himself. Intellectually she had understood that his memory and ability to care for himself had diminished but at an emotional level she still expected him to be as dignified and in command of himself as he had always been.

Expectations of Yourself

In all likelihood, you will have to adjust your expectations of yourself, as well as of your parents. Include yourself in your honest appraisal. You may find that you are more limited than you hoped, that you cannot meet all your parents' needs. Reluctant though you may be to admit it, other demands on your time and attention are often more of a priority. Being all things to all people may be possible in the very short run, but over time, you will only keep going if you are able to recognize your limits. Look at all your circumstances, and take on only what you can manage.

It is important to recognize that even with the best of intentions, some of your goals may be unattainable. Your parents suffer many losses that cannot be replaced, disabilities that cannot be cured, and pleasures they can no longer enjoy. They may be too frail and sick to live out their days in their own homes, surrounded by loving families, free from discomfort, grief, and frustration. Resources are limited, few human beings are saints, and not all pain and unhappiness can be eased. You may have to let go of the notion that you are able to bring complete tranquility and comfort into your parents' lives.

Another unreachable goal is that you will be loving and calm at all times. Unending good humor is a rare characteristic even in ideal situations; caring for an infirm person tests the temper of most people, at least some of the time. Under trying conditions, lapses in patience are inevitable. Since guilt and self-abasement are rarely helpful, you will do better to apologize, to forgive yourself, and to think how you can reduce your level of stress.

When Parents and Children Do Not Like Each Other

Deciding how much to be involved is complicated when you do not feel affection for your parents. You wonder if you will feel guilty or have regrets after they have died. You may worry about how others judge you. Weigh all the circumstances — the *real* circumstances, not the ideal — and then ask yourself whether you are satisfied with what you are doing.

Donna tried to explain why she could not take care of her mother.

I've spent much of my life trying to get away from my mother.
Right now, it doesn't look as if I've succeeded. She's got to leave
her apartment because she can't manage alone any longer. And
there's no one to help but me. The only thing I want to do is run
away. I see my life being consumed by her just as it was when I
was a kid and she was drunk half the time. Just talking about it
makes me feel ill. But the problem is that I can't turn my back
on her. It would be easier if I could. My husband thinks I'm crazy
because she was such a loser of a mother that I don't owe her any-
thing. Maybe he's right, but here I am, trying to work out what I
can do.

I do have enough sense to know that I can't live with her, so
I've found a small place where she'll have all meals provided and
people around to help her. The move went better than I thought
it would. That was a relief, but I was surprised at how sad I felt.
It was odd to see her so passive and cooperative. In the old days,
she would have had plenty to say about everything.

Not all of you are fond of your parents. You may have a long
history of friction, with your parents so negligent, uncaring, or even
abusive that they lost your respect and affection long ago. Or your
estrangement may be related to their aging. The strains of old age
and effects of disease may have made them so irritable and critical
that it is hard to be with them.

It may be difficult but it is extremely important to assess your
feelings honestly before you decide what role you will play in their
care. Beware if you are swayed by how you think you *should* feel
or how you would *like* to feel. Actions based solely on "should" are
often disastrous for everyone. If you and your parents have rarely
managed a harmonious visit for more than a few days when they
were healthy and intact, you are unlikely to live together successfully. If your parents are persistently critical and impatient with your
children, prolonged periods of time together will probably not be
tolerable for you. Your sense of duty alone will not make a plan
work. The time for you to honestly assess your feelings is before you
make any decision. Clinging to a hope that you or your parents will
change, will, in all probability, make matters worse.

If true affection does not provide the motivation, there are ways
you can act responsibly despite your need to keep your distance from
your parents. Parents have no intrinsic right to be loved just because
they are parents or because they are old. But they *do* have a right
to appropriate care, to a safe and comfortable environment, to kind

and respectful treatment — even though you may not be able to personally provide it. You can employ others or organize community services to provide the necessary care, or support your siblings who are directly involved.

If you find that you are spending enormous amounts of your time with parents you have never felt close to, you might ask yourself some tough questions. Is your attention excessive, or is it driven by the need to win affection or appreciation from people who were never able to provide it? While many parents and children do grow closer as they age, no amount of self-sacrifice assures it. Providing too much care in an attempt to repair a bad relationship is likely to leave you disappointed and resentful that the approval you want remains elusive. The desire for a loving parent is compelling. In your efforts to attain that, you may go to extraordinary lengths only to find that no amount of sacrifice can create love where it is not. This may be the hardest thing to accept.

Setting Limits

Along with honest self-assessment, you need to constantly consider your limitations. How much can you do? In what ways can you help? What are the effects of giving help — on yourself, your partners, and your children? If your parents are needy, you need to answer these questions truthfully. Otherwise, you will feel exhausted and resentful before long.

The honeymoon was soon over, and Mom started to complain about the home. She couldn't understand the rules. She wanted to smoke anywhere and have her bath whenever she chose. The worst thing, though, was that she couldn't go to the store when she wanted to. So she called me several times a day to take her. There was always some item that she could not do without. At first I thought I'd take her out once a week when I did my own errands, but that didn't work. Whenever she had the impulse to go out, she reached for the phone and was mad if I couldn't take her that moment.

I was going crazy. I told her not to call me at work, that I was busy. Why did I think she'd suddenly become thoughtful when she never had been? So I knew I had to do something different, or I'd really hate her.

The staff were not sympathetic — they had classified me as a negligent daughter, I think — but they did agree to try to discour-

age Mom from using the phone while I was at work. At home, I used the answering machine more.

I don't know what made the difference exactly, but she's a lot better now. I can't believe it, but I even volunteer to take her out sometimes — and enjoy it.

It is easy to see that your parents are restricted in what they can do as their strength decreases and their senses fail, but you have limits too. Yours are probably imposed by lack of time, energy, and patience. You may hope that your parents will see that you are pressed and modify their requests accordingly, but unfortunately people are not always so thoughtful, especially where their own interests are in conflict. Your mother may sympathize that you have to find time to drive your children to sports events but demand that you drive her to the grocery store. Recognizing your capacities and working within them is probably the best thing you can do for yourself.

The first step is to recognize that you have a *right* to draw some boundaries around what you do. You do not have to accept unreasonable demands on your time or abilities. Setting limits now may be a necessity if you are to continue to help your parents in the long term.

You may have parents who are abusive. They may have been critical and insensitive all your life. Some parents become more demanding as they try to deal with the limitations imposed by their physical disabilities. Helpless to fetch a drink for themselves or drive their own car, they may become unreasonably demanding of others. Some develop a dementing illness that may destroy their ability to handle frustration in any way other than with verbal or physical violence. Whether their behavior is deliberate or not, you have a right to protect yourself and to make it clear that there are limits to how you will allow yourself to be treated. If you quietly but firmly say, "I don't like to be yelled at. If you continue, I will leave," your parents will probably calm down. But, if not, do leave the room.

At the opposite extreme, your parents may use excessive gratitude or material rewards to keep you near them. "What would I do without you; you make me so happy" is more difficult to resist than complaints or criticism. Such a comment may be an expression of genuine feeling, but it can sometimes be manipulative. If you feel uncomfortable, that is a good sign that you may either be giving help your parents do not need or that you do not want to give.

Rather than acceding automatically to your parents' requests, it is worth looking at the consequences of saying yes. Evaluate the advantages and disadvantages, even if this means delaying the answer with "I'd like to think about it." Agreeing to pay a visit or help with a chore may not be your chosen way to spend a weekend, but after weighing what you and your parents might gain and lose, you may decide it is a good idea. You give up some time at home, but know that your attention means a great deal to your parents. The problem begins if your "yes" is reluctant. Then your irritation is likely to spill over, souring the visit for both of you. It is better to figure that out before you leave home. Here again is an occasion for honest self-assessment.

Why is it so difficult to say "no" to even unreasonable demands, especially when they come from parents? Most often, you probably agree to do things you do not want to do because you are at some level afraid — afraid of displeasing, of being criticized, of being thought selfish, of hurting your parents' feelings. And then you feel guilty that you are not a good son or daughter. When you confront these fears, you will find they lose some of their power. They are not so daunting that you need to avoid them at all costs. Is it so awful to be considered selfish on occasion? To be criticized? To have your parents disappointed or irritated for a while? It may be more important that you take some care of yourself. Then, when you help, you do so with good grace.

Once you know your limits and decide to pay attention to them, here are some useful guides.

At the beginning, lay the groundwork by being specific about what you can and cannot do. You may decide, for example, that you are willing to talk to your mother only once a day. Her telephone calls that come whenever she feels lonely or has a question are disruptive to your work and time with your family. It is considerate to tell your parents of your decision and your reasons for it. Sometimes they understand and make an effort to be less demanding. But even if they are unwilling or unable to cooperate, you have at least made it clear that you are making a change.

Secondly, many an argument can be prevented by using "I" messages. It is much more effective to make statements about yourself rather than comment negatively on your parents' behavior. "I know that you are lonely and like to talk but I find it difficult to do my work when you keep phoning me" is direct and honest. "You don't need to keep phoning me" is usually heard as critical, lacking in understanding, and much more likely to provoke an argument.

The words you chose, and especially the tone you use, are important. Introduce your plan in a thoughtful, respectful manner. "I've been thinking that the way we've been doing things is not working for me because...." When you decide to limit what you do, your parents are not likely to welcome your decision, but they may be more agreeable if you give your reasons and if you seem to understand how they feel. If you propose a dramatic change in direction, try to acknowledge your understanding of the effect on them. When you have visited your parents daily for several months and then decide you cannot continue to do so, it is fair to take responsibility for setting up that expectation and apologize for changing the rules. "I'm sorry I led you to expect to see me every day, but I find I can't keep that up."

By setting limits, you are depriving your parents of something they want. There may be positive aspects, however. Returning to the example of frequent telephone calls, you may need to restrict the number of times you speak on the phone, but you can improve the quality of the conversation. Your parents may willingly trade several perfunctory conversations for one that is more relaxed. A plan that often works well is to prearrange a time and day that is convenient for you both. "If we could plan to talk on Sunday mornings, I would be free to have a longer chat." If your parents are lonely, their anticipation of the conversation extends the benefits over several hours or even days.

When trying to alter any behavior, moderation is one key to success. One change at a time is easier for your parents to adjust to and for you to implement. If your parents are demanding and you have never taken care of yourself, your stress may have reached a high level. You find fault everywhere. Tempting though it is to try to make global improvements, you are more likely to be successful if you put your energy into one area at a time. Choose one irritation that, if changed, would make a clear difference to you. Ask yourself, what is one thing that would bring significant relief? Your parents' litany of complaints that seem to make up every conversation? Your parents' criticism of your children's manners? Lack of privacy? Keeping the greatest chance of success in mind, select a small problem to work on. It is easier to concentrate on some specific remedy, such as an evening out each week, than to tackle some broad concern, such as your parents' generally negative outlook.

If your parents have a dementing illness, it is more difficult to prevent yourself from becoming overburdened. Even in the early stages of the illness, when your parents still live alone, they may become excessively demanding because they have lost ability to be considerate, to moderate or even delay what they want. Recognize what they cannot manage and see that someone takes on those responsibilities — appointments, groceries, bills. You need to make sure they have what they need, but you do not have to meet every need yourself. Most chores and errands can wait. Try to use one visit to check on several items — that they have eaten breakfast, taken medication, have sufficient food in the refrigerator. Because they have little ability to absorb information, you will have to reiterate your routine frequently. Write your schedule and post it in an obvious place. A persistently repeated message may get through, especially if you use the same words each time. You will be less frustrated if you remember that your parents are not intentionally being difficult.

Acceptance of any change takes time and energy. And it demands as much from you as your parents. Perhaps more. You have to alter the way you do things and endure the feelings that arise. As you suggest a new plan and start to carry it out, your parents will press to stay with what is familiar. Habits die hard, but if you persist, new habits will replace old ones.

Sometimes, no amount of verbal insistence can persuade your parents to recognize your limitations. More drastic measures may be called for. If your parents fail to respect your reasonable wish that they limit the number or timing of their telephone calls, you may have to use an answering machine. If your parent is physically or verbally abusive, it is appropriate for you to say that you find their behavior offensive, and then leave if it continues.

Eventually, everyone benefits from setting necessary limits. You can continue to help because you are not overwhelmed, and your parents can feel that your care is given willingly.

Scapegoating and Elder Abuse

An occasional but tragic result of family conflict and stress is scapegoating and abuse. Although abuse of the elderly receives little attention in the media, many professionals believe that it is widespread and on the increase.

Scapegoating is a process of blaming others for problems for which they have little or no responsibility. Typically a scapegoat is a weak member of a group, weak because of age, health, or capabilities. Because children and frail elderly are dependent and need care from the generation in the middle, they are the vulnerable members in families.

Caring for elderly parents creates stress. For many caregivers, it is one stress among many. Other stresses may be more severe — financial worries, a poor marriage, deteriorating health, troublesome teenage children — but sometimes elderly parents receive a disproportionate amount of the blame. Troubled families, attributing their problems to their elderly parents, may inquire about nursing home care, not because their parents need that level of care, but because other issues are more difficult to deal with. One of my clients was distressed because her husband was pressing her to place her mother in a nursing home. In his opinion, her irritability was caused by the amount of time she had to spend with her mother. My client, however, liked to spend time with her mother, who showed an interest in her and clearly appreciated her. She felt loved and valued. Her husband was the one she found difficult.

Short of being blamed for others' problems, scapegoats sometimes become the target of negative feelings that belong elsewhere. You may not blame your fatigue or ill temper on your father, but nevertheless you may vent it on him. At the end of a tiring day it is only too easy to unload anger and frustration onto someone who is available and too vulnerable or dependent to answer back.

Abuse is scapegoating carried to an extreme. It takes several forms — physical, verbal, financial, and neglect. It is more likely to happen when caregivers are chronically fatigued and resentful, especially toward the people in their care, when they rely on drugs or alcohol, when they are under considerable stress from other difficulties, and, most important of all, when they have a history of angry outbursts. At the receiving end, most older people who are abused are very old women, frail, often irritable and demanding, and related to their caregivers. It is a disturbing fact that most elderly victims are abused by members of their own family. Some families have never learned to handle their problems in any other way except by yelling, insulting, or even hitting. Where there are dependent family members helpless to leave or protect themselves, such behavior can have tragic consequences. If you become so tense that you are in danger of acting out your anger, either by abusing or neglecting your parents, seek help immediately.

Elderly people who live alone are sometimes the targets of a different type of abuse. They can become the prey of unscrupulous manipulators intent on their own financial gain. If your parents are isolated and lonely they are particularly vulnerable to callers who pose as friendly and often charming people, offering to buy possessions or sell insurance, under the guise of helpfulness. Your parents are so grateful for the interest and companionship that they fail to see, or choose to ignore, that they are being used. They should be warned against any financial deals, whether offered over the telephone or in person, and encouraged to check with you before agreeing to anything. They are at less risk from people who come to the door if they have regular visitors themselves and are known by their neighbors. You may be able to reduce your parents' isolation by meeting their acquaintances and advocating a network of people to watch out for each other.

Points to Consider

1. Make your expectations of your parents and yourself as realistic as possible. Look at the situation honestly.

2. If you and your parents do not get along, take that into consideration when designing plans for their care.

3. If you find yourself thinking in terms of "should" or "ought," take a second look at your plans.

4. You do not have to accept unreasonable demands on your time and energy. Nor do you have to accept abuse.

5. Know what you are capable of doing and be clear to your parents about your limits.

6. When making changes in what you do, be fair to your parents. Explain why and what you are doing. Be consistent and resist temptations to return to old ways.

7. Abuse includes neglect, yelling, and rough handling as well as hitting. Seek help if you behave abusively in any way.

· Chapter 9 ·

Reconciling the Differences

HARD THOUGH your parents' old age is in many ways, it also brings some gifts. They may not be easy to see, especially while you are in the throes of concern for your parents, but they are there. And you have the power to receive them, or not.

The same frailties that introduce difficulties and loss also carry opportunities for growth. You may be able to use your parents' old age to grow closer to them and your siblings. You can become more comfortable with the differences between you. You can find things to appreciate. Time is running out. If you have not already done so, you can choose to let go of past differences and disappointments, you can attend to unfinished business, you can work for more intimacy. The bonds between you and your family may never be all that you wish for, but, as you cannot ignore them, it is worth putting thought into making them as satisfying as possible. With compassion for everyone, including yourself, you may be able to gain comfort from what you do have and, in doing so, perhaps tap a more satisfying level in those relationships.

Accepting What Is

Debbie's relationship with her mother had a rocky history.

I was depressed when my sister phoned to say Mom was in the hospital again. I knew that meant she would be moving in with us. For various reasons, my other sisters can't help out. I suppose these things never come at a good time, but my husband and I had just retired and we were really looking forward to some time to ourselves at long last. Unfortunately, Mom and I don't get on well. We don't fight or anything like that; we're just not close and I feel she always judges me harshly.

160

To give Mom credit, she managed the move well. She can be pretty self-centered, but she's not self-pitying. She accepted the fact she couldn't live alone any longer and didn't waste time on useless regrets. But neither did she show any sign that she was thinking of me and what this meant to my life. I don't suppose it occurred to her that I might not welcome the idea of her living with me. I didn't do as well. My fuse was really short. Everything irritated me.

I didn't realize how bad I was feeling until my daughter asked why I was so tense. She gets on very well with my mother — so does my husband. They can see that she's critical but they just laugh it off. They can't understand why I react so.

To be quite honest, I behave toward her the same as she behaves to me. I don't show her any affection either, or make a real effort to have a good conversation. It's a pity that we don't seem to bring out the best in each other. We'll probably never be close — that's the way it is — but I've decided it's a waste of energy to stay this angry.

It would be wonderful if we could all — parents, children, and siblings — have a nourishing relationship with each other. In reality, we often get on less well with members of our family than we would like. You may be bored by your relatives, with little to talk about. You may be tense around each other, expecting criticism or unwanted advice. You may long for affection but be afraid to give or ask for it.

Our feelings about each other are colored by what has happened in our past. History is a powerful force in families. What we learned as children stays with us, affecting the way we see ourselves and the way we react to others for the rest of our lives. If you, as a child, felt less loved than your brothers and sisters, you will probably, even as an adult, expect less attention from your parents, while at the same time desperately hoping for more. If you were the clown of the family, you may not be taken seriously by your siblings, even though you are now a responsible adult. You may grow indifferent to the reactions of your family but, more often, you become increasingly sensitive to signs from them that reinforce your expectations. Rather than resigned, you may be more easily provoked to anger, resentment, or depression. Debbie had become so sensitive to being criticized by her mother that she heard disapproval where her daughter heard only a question or an opinion.

Acutely aware of every nuance, you react in ways that have become well practiced over the years. Such patterns are firmly entrenched and are difficult to change. Difficult but not impossible.

A sense of history is useful because it can throw light on the present, but all too often the past is used to excuse the continuation of animosity or hopelessness. People hold on to past rivalries, jealousies, and injustices and use them to justify and fuel present discontents. Understanding where your feelings come from is not productive if you use it to stay in a bog of self-pity and recrimination. Rather, use it to help you take responsibility for charting your own course.

There comes a time when you may be ready to let go of those feelings that do nothing but open wounds. The past cannot be rewritten. An unhappy childhood will usually always be remembered as unhappy. People come with a range of strengths and weaknesses. If you are unlucky enough to have parents with more inadequacies than gifts and siblings who do not take their share of responsibilities, you are doomed to frustration if you persist in waiting for them to change. You cannot make your parents more loving or your siblings better friends. Anger and criticism are always damaging, never productive. It is wiser for you to put energy into accepting that your family members are limited — as we all are — and unable to give all that you would like. Each member of your family has many dimensions — not all good, not all bad — some of which you can regret, some appreciate.

Reworking the Relationship

The fact that old age ends in death may be the most powerful motive to look at how you connect with your parents. Time is limited and it no longer makes sense, if it ever did, to put off resolutions to talk about sensitive matters or to express what you feel. However apprehensive or shy you are, it is worth pushing yourself to express what you want your parents to know. This is the time to take emotional risks.

I don't know when I began to feel a little better about Mom, but I do. We still have our moments — plenty of them — but in general she is less difficult to please. And I'm less irritable.

It's an odd thing that brought us closer. Mom needs me to wash her hair — she just doesn't have the strength. I'd forgotten how much I used to love her hair when I was a kid — it was gorgeous, long and thick. Occasionally, if she was in a good mood, she'd let me brush it. Her hair isn't gorgeous any longer, but I still like fussing with it — and she likes it too.

You can make changes in your relationships within your family if you really want to. Depending on the circumstances and personalities involved, the changes may be small, but significant nonetheless. As your parents grow frail, you may have more contact with all members of your family, which in itself gives you opportunities to do things differently. You can choose how you regard your time together — as a duty, a bore, or as a chance to get to know each other better.

One client of mine used an unpromising situation to enrich his relationship with his father. His father needed the care of a nursing home. The best available home happened to be in the town where he, the youngest son, worked. As other members of the family lived at some distance, it fell to him to be his father's regular visitor. Although he had become a store owner like his father, the two of them had never been close. Visiting his father in the nursing home was awkward. They had rarely talked and now his father's dementia made conversation almost impossible. One day, on an impulse, the son took his father to his store. He had rarely seen his father look so happy. He was clearly in familiar surroundings as he wandered among the shelves or sat by the cashier. After that, the visits became a regular weekly event, and father and son found new pleasure in each other's company.

Crisis often brings about change by necessity rather than by choice. When everything is in a state of flux, the changes can result in good developments. Your parents may suffer sudden health problems, need to be cared for, or have to move house. In each situation, you face dilemmas and confront decisions that are invariably unwelcome. At the same time, you may discover strengths and competencies that please and surprise you. You and your parents may begin relating to each other differently.

Change is rarely easy. With time and work, however, you may come to see old hurts and quarrels from a less painful perspective. It is important to see your parents as people with their own struggles and frailties. If you are prepared to listen and refrain from insisting on the rightness of *your* opinion, you may gain some understanding or compassion for your parents' point of view. Fortunately, changes do not have to be major to make a difference. Small shifts in attitude, as with Debbie and her mother, have a significant impact on a relationship. Simple changes of behavior, as with my client and his father, can open new avenues of communication.

Sometimes past hurts were so severe that they retain all their pain. If this is so for you, you may have to recognize that you will never have an acceptable relationship with your parents. Your challenge will be to come to terms with your anger and grief, and handle your feelings in a way that ensures that the past does not constantly infect the present. You have two choices: you can be resentful, reinjuring yourself as you relive a bitter past, or you can accept what exists and do the best you can with it.

Siblings Too

As your parents need assistance, you will probably have more contact with your brothers and sisters. And it may be a different kind of contact than you have had to date. For the first time, you may have to share responsibilities and make joint decisions. Depending on your ability to work together, you may come to appreciate each other more, or you may grow further apart.

Many people who care for their parents report that of all their relationships, those with their brothers and sisters are especially stressful. For some, resentments that began in childhood deepen as your parents need help and you see siblings either failing to do their share or being treated in a preferential way.

You and your siblings have had many developmentally tender years to get to know each other well. By adulthood, you may have become accustomed to being let down, overlooked, not heard. You are not only sensitive to hurts from your brothers and sisters but you may even anticipate them. Locked into old patterns of behavior, you may find it difficult to hope that your relationship could be different. If you have always felt vulnerable with your siblings, it may feel too risky to assert your point of view. If you have always felt like the responsible member of the family, you may fail to ask for help, assuming that the others are incapable or unwilling to lend a hand. You may complain to others about your uncaring or selfish brothers and sisters but be completely incapable of addressing the situation with them. In this way, relationships among siblings can reach an uncomfortable impasse.

Like most brothers and sisters you probably do not have a procedure for negotiating your differences. When you are annoyed with each other you tend to return to the patterns of childhood. If you felt powerless then, as adults you may shrug and do nothing; if you felt picked on, you may retreat and be resentful; if you felt strong, you may state opinions with some degree of insensitivity. You do not often say aloud such thoughts as "It's not fair," "It's your turn; I did it last time," "You were always the favorite," but sometimes you may come close. It does not require a large leap of imagination to picture yourself and your siblings back in time, as children squabbling over whose turn it is to do the dishes. Life's circumstances change people, often making them more confident and competent, but siblings frequently experience a time warp that tends to pull everyone back to old ways.

However, the changes in your parents that may bring these difficulties to the surface can also provide the impetus to handle things differently. Your parents' sudden ill health may encourage a sibling who has been on the fringe of the family to move back in, or another to demonstrate more competence than anyone thought possible. If a member of your family takes an unexpected and positive step, the response of the rest of you does much to determine whether or not it is successful. When you show each other some compassion, persist in trying to include rather than exclude, and do not put energy into maintaining old complaints, you will probably find yourselves growing closer. Your parents' old age may or may not bring forth unexpected strengths. Keeping a mind open to that possibility enhances the chance of good change happening.

We all expend energy on thinking about how others can change, but, of course, the only people we have any control over are ourselves. Your siblings may continue to behave as they always have, but if you change the way you react, the situation will be different. As much as you are able, engage with your siblings as adults rather than as the children you once were. When you are affected by past resentments, which inevitably you will be, register them, but leave them in their place rather than allow them to spoil the present. Tempting though it may be to score points off your siblings, try to avoid their vulnerabilities. Think about engaging them in ways that will make it easier for them to behave as adults. If you strive to support each other in the care of your parents, you will be more aware of what you mean to one another. Your relationship will, at least, be more appreciative and, at best, be enriched, bringing pleasure to all.

Unfinished Business

I don't know how much longer Mom will last. Her emphysema is putting quite a strain on her heart. I realized there were some things we needed to know, such as where she wanted to be buried, or, come to that, would she prefer to be cremated. I didn't know how to bring up these topics. Fortunately, my husband didn't have a problem. Once he'd broken the ice, and I could see that Mom didn't get upset, I got into the discussion. It wasn't so difficult.

Mom and I are certainly talking about more these days. I've learned things about her life — and mine when I was little — that she'd never talked about before. We were never close enough to really talk, except for her to criticize me — so it seemed to me. I always felt she didn't love me. I'd like to ask her about that — I think — but I'm not sure that I can. Perhaps one day.

As your parents feel old, they often begin to think about the business they want to complete before they die. They want to sort through belongings, put papers in order, decide how to distribute special possessions. For them, this is the work of a responsible person, a tidying up. For you, the emotional meaning is loud and clear, and you may not want to hear it. It is a strangely disjointed experience to discuss with your parents plans and policies that will be carried out only when they are no longer alive. Their belongings are part of them and not easily separated. Your talk may sound dispassionate, but you are both aware of preparing for an ending. For your parents, your interest and willingness to help are important beyond the practical.

Emotional business is even more complicated. As there is no way of knowing exactly how and when your parents will die, just that they will, it will serve you well to think about what you want to say to them before death is imminent. Here is a useful question to pose to yourself: "If I had but one chance to see my parents again, what would I ask, do, or say?" It is not only death that cuts off communication. With modern medicine's ability to keep bodies alive, most people's brains become impaired before their bodies finally cease to function. Do not wait until it is too late to say what is important, whether it is asking a question, conveying your feelings, or saying goodbye. In any case, if something is worth saying, sooner is usually better than later. Why waste valuable time that might be spent enjoying a more affectionate or, at least, understanding relationship?

Like you, your parents may have loose emotional ends to tie up — love and thanks they have not expressed, subjects they have avoided, rifts they have not mended. They may find it difficult to talk about their feelings, especially if they have rarely done so, and their efforts may be clumsy or timid enough to go unheeded. Or they may express what they feel indirectly in the form of an invitation or a gift or by praising your children. You can help by being aware of their attempts to build bridges, and reaching out to meet them.

Reconstituting the Family

When Mom died, the whole family gathered. It's strange that it takes a death to bring everyone together. I looked around at the funeral and wondered if it would ever happen again. I'd see my sisters again — no doubt about that as we've got closer over the time Mom has been living with me — but I don't know about my brothers. It's easy to drift apart when both your parents are dead. And we've never had much in common.

But they are family and I can't imagine not caring at all. I don't know how I feel. I do know they won't initiate getting together. Perhaps I'll make the first move. Since Mom came to me, I've become something of the head of the family. Perhaps I'll talk to my sisters about coming for Thanksgiving this year, and inviting the boys.

The bond between siblings is like no other, made up as it is of shared parents, surroundings, and memories stretching over many years. You may have become genuine friends with your brothers and sisters, a relationship to which your common experience adds a special level of understanding. Even if you do not much like each other, you probably feel some attachment.

Your parents' death puts your relationship with your siblings into sharp relief. It has to be appraised on its own merits. What relationship do you want? Are you such good friends that there is no doubt that you will choose to spend time together? Is there now no reason to meet? Or do you fall in the middle position — wanting to maintain some connection, but not enjoying joint visits enough to make them a high priority?

While your parents were alive, they were probably the hub around which you, your siblings, and your children spent time together. There were traditional family times and places. Even when they became unable to organize family events, your parents' physical presence and need for care continued to provide focus for your interaction with each other. Who takes over this role when parents die? Sometimes nobody does. Death breaks the fragile bond that stayed in place only as long as your parents were alive. More often, a new family system evolves almost without anyone being conscious of it.

Following the informal rules that have developed over many years of living as a family, one person, such as the oldest sister, becomes the head and others allow that to happen. That person or any other family member may then take the initiative in suggesting family get-togethers. And when you do get together, you may do so in the time-honored ways your family always did, or you may develop new, more satisfying traditions.

Points to Consider

1. You do have some control over the quality of your relationship with others.

2. If there is tension between you and your parents or you and your siblings, check the probability that you contribute to that.

3. If you feel bitter about the way your parents or siblings treated you, it may be time to let go of your anger. Leave the past behind and live as fully as you can in the present.

4. Keep an open mind about other family members. They may want to try to help, even though they have not done so in the past.

5. Consider how you can use the crises and difficulties of your parents' old age as an opportunity for change and personal growth.

6. Give yourself credit for changes you make, however small, and note their impact is often important.

7. Think about what you want to ask or say to your parents before they die. If you want to express your appreciation or love, do it now.

8. Your parents' old age is an opportunity for you and your siblings to work together, support each other, and grow closer.

9. If you want to maintain contact with your siblings after your parents have died, take the initiative. Parents' deaths leave a vacuum that may remain if you wait for others to make the first move.

· *Chapter 10* ·

The Final Letting-Go

❧

G RIEVING IS A PROCESS, a painful process, that follows the rupture of any important relationship. We humans — and some other animals — have the capacity to care for things outside ourselves. Status, possessions, dreams, activities, are important to varying degrees, but relationships with other human beings matter most to us. When these connections are broken, we are often extremely distressed. When a relationship that meant a great deal ends, grief is the emotion we deal with. It is the inevitable result of caring about others. At times, the pain of loss may seem intolerable, but the capacity for affection and attachment is a precious part of being human. Without it, we are somehow stunted.

Of all endings, the death of a parent is the one most likely to be passed over by others as without much significance. After all, people say, death is an inevitable part of old age. It is a reason for sadness, but not too much or for too long. For most, a parent's death does not disrupt life in the way that the loss of a spouse or child does. Nevertheless, it can be deeply affecting. Whether the ending came suddenly or was expected, whether your relationship was close or distant, the death of your parent is not a minor loss.

Grief

Grief for someone close to you is complex, containing many different feelings, some of them uncomfortable. You may be relieved that your parent's suffering and your caregiving is over, sad that someone important to you is gone, accepting that a long life was ready to end, or regretful that your relationship was not more satisfying. Your emotions are profound and sometimes conflicting.

While most of us experience similar feelings, the pattern of grief is essentially a personal one. Just as each human relationship is unique, so is each person's grief. There is no right or wrong method, no set timetable, no collection of correct emotions. Your mourning may be anguished or so quiet that it goes almost unnoticed by others; it may be brief or prolonged, come quickly or be delayed; it may contain feelings of relief and anger, as well as sadness.

Many factors influence how you react. Did your parents die after a long illness, or suddenly? Were they very old or too young? Were they ready to die or still enjoying life? What was your relationship like? Ironically, grief may be more prolonged when you and your parents were dissatisfied with each other or left many things unsaid or unresolved. Regret and resentment can persist for a long while, whereas the sadness at losing a good relationship may be more quickly replaced by happy memories. Did the death come alone or have you had other recent losses? Your parents may have died within a short period of each other, leaving you orphaned and doubly bereaved. What about your personality? Do you express your feelings openly, turn to friends for support, or keep your pain inside? These and many other circumstances affect your mourning.

When you think of grief, you probably picture sadness and tears. You may experience numerous other symptoms, however, many of them physical, and in varying degrees of intensity. We tend to think of our minds as distinct from our bodies, but strong emotions leave no doubt that body and mind are really part of the same system, not separate entities. Our bodies reflect how we feel. In the intense phase of your grief, you will probably have troubled sleep and a poor appetite, and you may feel fatigued and vaguely unwell. You may keep some of these physical sensations for some time, especially your lack of energy and interest, even for things that you used to enjoy. Not only are you sad, but you feel empty and unmotivated because nothing has meaning.

At first, many things remind you of your parent — a particular food, a certain smell, the sight of an old person on the street. You may find yourself crying without warning. You may think of your parent frequently, often ruminating about what you wish you had said or done. It usually helps to talk, so seek out friends who listen well and members of your family whose memories and grief support your own.

Gradually, the pain subsides and your parents live on in your happier memories.

Shock and Denial

If your parents died suddenly, your immediate feelings are of shock and denial. You experience a sense of disbelief, that it cannot be true, that some mistake must have been made. Often you have little emotion, rather a sensation of acting like a robot. This denial serves a useful purpose as it allows you to let in bad news at a pace you can absorb, without being overwhelmed. Without it, you would probably be unable to attend to all the necessary practical details. The numbness often lasts until after the funeral; only then are you hit by waves of sadness. Looking back on those early days, you may be amazed at what you accomplished, because you can remember little about it.

Grief in Anticipation

If your parents had been ailing for some time or are very old, their death comes as less of a shock. You have had time to think about life without them, to rehearse, as it were, what that will be like. This is sometimes called "anticipatory grief." Your grieving started when they first became seriously ill or began to fail and change. It is a prolonged process as you mourn each loss, each sign of decline. There may have been several medical emergencies where death appeared imminent, only to be postponed for a while longer. Or life may have been slowly slipping away for weeks, or months, with the boundary between life and death becoming less and less distinct. Death preceded by prolonged dying exacts its own emotional toll, which is often more wearing than one occurring without warning, but it is usually less overwhelming and disruptive when it finally occurs.

But you cannot do all your grieving ahead of time. However well prepared you think you are for your parents' death, you may be surprised how upsetting it is. Allow yourself to feel your feelings.

Relief

One of the tragedies of a long decline is that both you and your parents are sometimes ready for a death that refuses to come. When it finally arrives, your strongest feeling may be one of relief — relief that your parents' suffering is finished, relief for yourself that your burden is over. Normal though your reaction is, you may be shocked by it.

Long illnesses often so erode the quality of life that you may wish that your parents would die. If they have a slow-moving, disabling illness, such as Alzheimer's disease, you probably pray that they succumb to some swift and kinder condition rather than endure a disease that seems to go on interminably. Modern medicine is adept at extending the length of life but not always the quality. At the end, when more medical care is provided than at any other time, you can be on an emotional roller coaster as your failing parents go from one health crisis to another. Extended medical treatment, and especially nursing home care, can ravage your family's finances, as well as your emotional endurance. It is difficult to admit that you wish your parents' lives to be over, but there comes a point when death is welcome, relieving them of an existence that holds only pain, disability, or confusion, and you of continued distress.

Sadness

Sadness is the main feature of any grief, and a feeling that you all expect to have. It is made up of many components. If you have been fortunate, you will miss your parents' love and support that nurtured you as a child and has followed you into adulthood. If you have never had that kind of love, you feel sad because now you will never have it. While your parents were alive, there was some hope that they would finally show some approval or affection, but death removes that hope.

You may also miss the relationship you developed with your parents as adults. As you have grown older, many of you have become close, but in a different way than when you were young. You may have become friends. If you are single and have not yet established your own home, you may lose your primary family when your parents die.

If your parents had a chronic, dementing illness, your sadness is for what you lost years ago. Death itself probably came as no surprise and with some relief, but your pain is that you can only remember your parents as they were at the end — a deteriorated shell of what they used to be. It takes time, but you will begin to picture your parents as the vital people they were for most of their lives.

Although your sadness diminishes over the months, it does return on occasions, such as births, graduations, or weddings, that particularly remind you of your parents and that you long to share with them. Their death leaves an empty place at such celebrations. Do not be afraid to bring their name into the gathering, to wish they were there. If you miss them, it is more than likely that others do too.

Guilt

Most people who are grieving feel some guilt whether they have reason for feeling it or not. A large percentage of those who have cared for their parents and by any reasonable standard have been responsible and loving report that after their parents have died, they felt badly that they did not do more. Guilt does not always have a sound basis. Rather, it indicates that people rarely live up to their own expectations. They demand of themselves that they are patient, cheerful, available 100 percent of the time. Having an ideal may be laudable but falling short of it is inevitable.

You may be haunted by your parents' last few days, wishing you had said something different, done more, been more kind. If your relationship was a distant or difficult one, you may criticize yourself that you did not make more efforts to close the gap, to help whenever you were needed, to visit even when inconvenient. Even those of you who were attentive, however, may feel some regret that you did not make that extra effort or were not successful in relieving your parents' suffering. If you can accept that you have limitations and that some errors of judgment are unavoidable, you are less likely to spend energy on feeling critical of yourself. Instead, appreciate what you were able to do.

Anger

Anger is another of those feelings, like relief, that is not seen as quite acceptable when talking about the death of people you love. Yet you may well have this feeling. You have lost, you have been left, and you can do nothing about it. If your parents had taken better care of themselves, they might still be alive. If they had been more organized, you would not have so many of their problems to sort out. If one parent had not died, you would not have responsibility for the other.

More commonly, your anger is focused, not on the person who has died, but on others — on members of the medical profession for providing inadequate care, on your siblings for being autocratic or unhelpful, on your remaining parent for being demanding or difficult, on God for allowing it to happen. Such anger is sometimes justified — doctors do make mistakes, people are insensitive — but often your anger comes from your helplessness to do anything except watch your parent die. Your tension is such that you may explode at those who should be able to help.

However competent and loving their care, your parents may be in pain, confused and unaware of their surroundings. They may be hooked up to machines that make it difficult to be close to them, physically or emotionally. They are often unable to talk or even recognize that you are with them. Watching from the bedside, you are angry that they are not able to die as they would have wished — without suffering and with dignity.

Under many circumstances, anger is natural. If you recognize what you are feeling, and why, your anger does not have to be the negative reaction you fear.

Typically, your intense feelings of grief fade after a few months. Although you will continue to feel sad, your distress noticeably lessens. Do not grade your progression through your mourning by comparing yourself with what you read or think you see in others. You, your relationship, your situation are different from any other, and so is your reaction to a death. Give yourself the time and space to give your feelings full expression in whatever way is appropriate and helpful to you.

If, after several months, you remain preoccupied by your loss and unable to find your usual pleasure and interest in life, you would probably find it useful to talk to a professional counselor.

As your grieving diminishes, you will regain your energy and enthusiasm for living. While your parent was sick, whether for a short or drawn-out period, you may have had your life on hold. If you were the caregiver, you may have experienced years of postponing plans and dismissing potential activities. The future gradually asserts its pull. It is yours to embrace.

Points to Consider

1. Grief is a normal feeling that accompanies the loss of someone you are attached to.

2. There is no right or wrong way to grieve. It is very personal. You will give yourself unnecessary distress if you compare your grief with others.

3. Grief is a complicated process. Don't ignore your less acceptable feelings, such as relief and anger.

4. Find people to talk to — people who understand what you are going through.

5. If grief persists over many months with little lessening of intensity, consider seeking professional help.

6. Life will reassert itself. Embrace it.

Final Word

You deserve full recognition for what you are doing for your parents. Whether you are providing care yourself, ensuring that others are doing so, or giving support at long distance, your contribution to your parents' welfare counts enormously. Without your help, your parents' lives would be more difficult on a practical level and poorer on an emotional one.

This book is primarily concerned with the "hows" of caring for your parents. How you decide what to worry about, when to take charge, how to talk to your parents, when to ask for help and from whom, how to take care of yourself. The list of these questions could be endless. There is a more fundamental question, however, that you might ask: why?

Why do you care for your parents? I believe that the answers you come up with will reveal the meaning behind what you do. Victor Frankl, whose branch of psychotherapy — logotherapy — developed during the terrible privations of the Nazi concentration camps, focused on helping people discover the meaning of their lives. "Life ultimately means taking the responsibility to find the right answer to its problems and to fulfil the tasks which it constantly sets for each individual." The answers that are uniquely yours are cornerstones of your character and indicators of your own greater sense of purpose. If you can see that the daily pressures of *how* you meet your responsibilities are *part* of what gives your life meaning, they will certainly be easier to endure. The wearying and trying details of what you do can acquire importance in the context of your larger purpose.

In caring for your parents you may be primarily motivated by love, by duty, or by gratitude. You may feel you are expressing God's love, following Fate's plan for you, or fulfilling your birthright's responsibility as a member of your family. You may be thinking of your own old age and wanting to be an example to your children. You may want to ensure that your parents live out their lives as fully and comfortably as possible. Probably you are influenced by many of these considerations, and others not mentioned.

Though you did not choose to be in the situation you are in, you *can* choose how you handle it. Hard though your job is at times, you can elect to make something positive of it. You can aim to manage it with dignity, empathy, and humor. You may falter often, but you always have the freedom to return to your resolution.

Any conditions that challenge us beyond our own comfortable way of being give us an opportunity to grow. Caring for your parents provides you with such an opportunity. Problems may seem constantly to call for more creativity, skill, and persistence than you think you can muster. Your patience, flexibility, and understanding may be taxed to the breaking point. When you look back, however, you will probably be surprised by the breadth of your capacities. You may brush your achievement aside with "What choice did I have?" or "Anyone would have done the same," but you deserve credit for what you did, and for doing as well as you were able. If thanks from others is not forthcoming, and very often it is not, remember to recognize your own efforts.

Most of us regard old age with some ambivalence. Looking ahead, it seems that life would be improved if that last stage did not exist. But life has its cycle. Just as there is no spring without winter, life without death, so there is no youth without old age. In caring for your parents you are not only easing their passage from this life but connecting yourself to all phases of life.

Many people have told me that caring for their parents has taught them some vital lessons. They become poignantly aware that if there are important things to say, feelings to express, and relationships to enjoy, it makes sense to attend to them now and not leave them until it seems too late. And they think about their own future decline, how they want to live, and especially how they can make life simpler for their children when the time comes that they themselves need care.

My hope for you is that you will gain something of real value from the experience of caring for your parents. You have responded with grace and generosity to another's need. You have done the best you could. You have endured upheavals you could not have anticipated. Your effort and your commitment have given meaning to your life and eased the struggle of those who gave life to you. Well done. Godspeed.

Of Related Interest...

Judah L. Ronch
ALZHEIMER'S DISEASE

"Whether a social worker or a family member, a professional caregiver or simply a friend, anyone who deals with the painful consequences of Alzheimer's will benefit from this exceptionally helpful and hopeful book."
—Dr. William Van Ornum
0-8245-1284-7 $12.95 pbk

Marylou Hughes
THE NURSING HOME EXPERIENCE
A Family Guide to Making It Better

"This an A to Z 'must read' for all concerned." — *Resources in Aging*
0-8245-1448-3 $11.95 pbk

Eugene Bianchi
AGING AS A SPIRITUAL JOURNEY

"How to grow old with grace, faith, and dignity...significant [and] useful."
— *Commonweal*
0-8245-0622-7 $16.95 pbk

Eugene Bianchi
ELDER WISDOM
Crafting Your Own Elderhood

More than a hundred older people, from Jimmy Carter to Tillie Olsen, share what they are learning along the way.
0-8245-1359-2 $21.95 hc

David A. Crenshaw
BEREAVEMENT
Counseling the Grieving throughout the Life Cycle

"A wealth of information...This book should prove extremely useful for those who want a practical guide for helping others handle bereavement." — *Booklist*
0-8245-1291-X $10.95 pbk

•

At your bookstore or to order directly from the publisher, please send check or money order (including $3.00 for the first book plus $1.00 for each additional book) to:

CROSSROAD
370 Lexington Avenue
New York, NY 10017

We hope you found *Caring for Elderly Parents* beneficial.
Thank you for reading it.